Romantic Spain

A Record of Personal Experiences

(Volume. I)

John Augustus O'Shea

Alpha Editions

This edition published in 2023

ISBN : 9789357941181

Design and Setting By
Alpha Editions
www.alphaedis.com
Email - info@alphaedis.com

Contents

PREFACE.

THIS simple recital of personal haps and mishaps in perturbed Spain from the abdication of Amadeus to the entry of Don Carlos, puts forward no claim to the didactic or dogmatic. Its chief aim is to amuse. Of course, if I succeed in conveying knowledge and dispelling illusions—in Tasso's words, if I administer a pill under a coating of jam—I shall be cock-a-hoop with delight. But I warn the reader I am not an unprejudiced witness. I am passionately fond of Spain and her people. Although years have elapsed since the events dealt with occurred, I fancy the narrative will not be hackneyed, for in Spain public life repeats itself with a fidelity which is never monotonous. I do not pretend to cast the horoscope of the poor little monarch who is in the nurse's arms, but Heaven guard him! 'Twere better for him that he had been born in a Highland shieling.

Should there be much individualism in these pages, it is intentional, and to be ascribed to the instance of friends. They said, "Bother history; give us plenty of your own experiences." It is to be hoped they have not led me astray by their well-meant advice.

CHAPTER I.

Which, being non-essential, treats partly of Spain, but principally of the Writer.

THE sun was shining with a Spanish lustre—a lustre as of glowing sarcasm—seeing that on that very day a Fire-Worshipper, Dadabhai Naoroji, was over-shadowed in his attempt to become a Member of Parliament for Holborn. The sun, I repeat, was shining with a Spanish lustre while the inquisition was being held. The tribunal was in the open air, under the mid plane-tree in Camberwell Green, the trimmest public garden in London. Conscience was the inquisitor, and the charge I had brought against myself was that of harbouring a vagrom spirit. I should have been born in a gipsy caravan or under a Bedaween's tent. Nature intended me to have become a traveller, a showman, or a knight-errant; and had Nature been properly seconded, I should have been doing something Burnabyish, Barnumesque, or Quixotic this afternoon, instead of sitting down on a bench between a tremulous old man in almshouse livery and a small boy fanning himself with a cap. Yes; I fear I must plead guilty. I am possessed by a demon of unrest; my soul chafes at inaction, calls aloud for excitement. Had I the ordering of my own fortune I should spread the white wings of a yacht to woo the faint wind (but it may be blowing freshly off the Foreland), or should vault on the back of a neighing barb with bushy mane and tail. But I am Ixion-lashed to the wheel of duty, leg-hampered by the log of necessity.

What is a gentle-born vagabond to do?

The law will not permit him to pink with his sword-stick the first smug fellow he meets on the side-path, self-respect debars him from highway-robbery which can be perpetrated without fear of the law, and it is idle to expect a revolution in this humdrum country within any reasonable period. A General Election which is going on, with its paltry show of coloured strips of calico, its printed appeals to the gullible, its occasional bits of ribbon and bursts of cheering, its egotisms, its stupidities, its self-seekings, its shabby intrigues and simulated fire, its dull, dreary, drivelling floods of witless substance in ungrammatical form—that, surely, is no satisfying substitute for the tumult of real political strife.

Motion is the sovereign remedy for the vagabond's disease, and lo! through the leafy barrier of the pollarded limes bordering the Green, jingle the bells of the tram-car with its trotting team of three abreast. Three mules, which bring my thoughts to Spain, and to a letter I have had from my publishers, satirically asking how soon they might expect the last pages of a promised book on the land of the Dons, the first line of which is not yet committed to paper. I must think over that book as I jog along the grooves of the street rails, and survey the prospect from the roof. How do those mules on the flanks manage to avoid knocking their hoofs against the metal-ruts, and tripping themselves up? What a stand-and-deliver air the conductor has as he presents his snip-snap apparatus, like the brutal key of the primitive dentist, and viciously punches an orifice in your ticket! For these conductors, as for letter-carriers, I have a profound sympathy; they are over-worked and under-paid; and yet they enjoy motion in abundance. But there is a poetry of motion, as when charging squadrons skim the plain, or a graceful girl with dainty ankles trips across the beeswaxed floor; and there is a prose of motion, as of a policeman plodding over his beat, or the Sisyphus-toil of the treadmill. I ask myself, Will a tram-conductor ever write a poem? Hardly, I think; and yet, why not? Was not Edward Capern, who achieved some smooth verses, a letter-carrier?

New Cross, our terminus so far. Over the way is another tram, which will take us to Greenwich for the outlay of another twopence. Shortly it will be one continuous avenue of pretentious masonry, from the Thames at Blackfriars to the Thames by the naval palace, instead of the former pleasant drive through Surrey fields. With what a fever they are building, terrace upon terrace, street upon street, interminable rows of villas in line or semi-detached! The patches of verdure, so refreshing to the jaded city eye, are diminishing in size and lessening in number. I like Greenwich; but they should never have removed the veterans of the ocean from it. Dear to the soul of youth, hankering for the strange and the stirring, were their three-cornered hats, their wooden stumps, their withered monkey-jaws puffed with quids, and their hoarse, squall-tearing voices. What a consuming thirst they had, and with what heroic industry they did tell lies! Peter of Russia was right: the sovereigns of England, the sea-rulers, should hold court in Greenwich. The Park with its fallow-deer is regal; the Painted Hall is eloquent with historic memories; the initial meridian is an imposing address; and then the Thames—but here, we are at it. A steamer awaits, and will carry us to the heart of London for a groat.

How dingy, dirty, despicable most of those steamers are! with their low-roofed, grimy cabins; their irritating hawkers of hat-strings and small beer; their stale stock of mawkish refections; their job-lot orchestras of wheeze and pipe and scrape and tootle; their smell of bilge and oil, sweat and cheap cigars, overtopped at holiday-times by the sulphurous oath or the rank obscenity of some reeling passenger. And yet how skilfully they thread their way through the crowded Pool; how readily they answer the wheel; with what ease they slow or quicken their run, and dart hither and thither; and with what nicety they are brought alongside the floating wharf! I wonder do the skippers of these boats move their hands in their dreams. Is the finger-sign for "Back her," that they use at home when they wish to replenish their pipes?

Collisions there may be, explosions there have been; but the career of the mariner who plies between Chelsea Pier and the port of Woolwich must be singularly free from such vicissitudes as shipwreck or failure of provisions; he is seldom caught in a tornado, or banged into by a privateer; he rarely knocks up against an iceberg, or gets a glimpse of the Flying Dutchman; sharks he may not study, except, perhaps, in the Westminster Aquarium, and when he dies he is trenched in commonplace clay. I cannot picture such a mariner to myself as having the spirit to ejaculate, "Shiver my timbers!"

The sight of a vessel from Seville laden with fruit and wine recalls me to that letter from the publishers and the book anent Spain. Not a word of it written yet. *They* will be shivering *my* timbers if I have it not ready in season. But I am not of those, like Anthony Trollope, who can sit down to their desks and turn out so many pages of copy at a stretch mechanically, much as a tinglary with its rotating handle grinds out a series of tunes. I cannot write unless I am in the mood, and that, I find, depends on the state of health and the absence of mental worry. The brain with some people refuses to become a piece of machinery. Of motion is often born inspiration—Hermes, god of oratory, is represented with *petasus* and *talaria*—and I am enjoying motion.

"Ease her—stop her!" Blackfriars Bridge, and here I quit the steamer's deck for the tram that will take me back to the place whence I came, and so enable me to have made a diversified circular tour by land and water for the expenditure of tenpence. Who would waste his substance on coach-men and high-steppers; who would envy Sir Thomas Brassey his lordly pleasure-craft, when this round of travel, with its buoyant sense of independence at the end, can be accomplished for tenpence? And now I shall hie me to a bar I wot of, and with the two pence that remain of my splendid shilling, I shall cheer the inner man with a clear, cool, mantling glass of foam-crowned bitter beer.

The beer ought to be good in Camberwell, for here Mrs. Thrale lived of yore, and the ponderous lexicographer took his walks, and mused on the vanity of human wishes. We have breweries still, and we have groves, even groves of Academus, where one may laugh; for are they not sacred to the shades of the two Hoods and Jeff Prowse, the "Nicholas" of *Fun*, as to Nick Woods, the Napier-recorder of Inkermann, and to associations with William Black, Henry Bessemer, and John Ruskin, master of art, which is something more, and more significant, than that *Magister Artium* which persons doubtful of their gifts or station ostentatiously affix to their names? And in our groves we have such variety of arborescent prizes as no other district of London can boast, extending to the arbutus or strawberry-tree, and the liriodendron or tulip-tree. The liriodendron has been planted in Palace Yard, in the hope that the breath of wholesomeness, genial to its native America, shall permeate the badly-ventilated atmosphere of the adjacent House of Commons. I love trees as if I were suckled by a hamadryad. May he who cuts them down to build whereon they stood taste the bitterness of Acheron!

And Camberwell Green, which I dearly affect, is it not replete with every modern convenience, as those ambitious amateurs who write the auction-bills are wont to phrase it? There is a bank where you may cash a cheque; two public-houses where you may spend great part of it fuddling yourself; a police-station where you may sleep the fuddle off; a pillar-box where a letter may be posted summoning a bail to your aid; a drinking-fountain where you may slake your thirst when you come out penitent from the police-office; a Turkish-bath, with a crescent-and-star daubed piece of bunting over it, where you may knead your frame into sobriety; a hairdresser's where you may make yourself presentable; a stationer's where my friend Morris will lavishly dose you with the tonic of moral apothegm; and, right opposite, a horse-trough where you may give yourself the ducking you deserve.

Inside the tavern, where I sought the beer, I met a financier, a shrewd fellow of a gross habit of body and a dry wit. He is accountant to a firm of book-makers, and can hold his own with the tongue; he married into the family of a late eminent prizefighter, and, with the connection, seems to have acquired the talent of holding his own with the fist. I like Wat much, and have obtained various scraps of desultory information from him which are useful.

Imprimis, that a penny ticket on a river-steamer on a Sunday constitutes a man as *bonâ fide* a traveller as Henry M. Stanley, and endows him with the privilege of getting liquid comfort within prohibited hours.

Item, that the cigars on the outside of a bundle, and therefore indented with the tape, are generally the best.

Item, that if there is hide or pelt on a carcase before a butcher's stall, you may take for granted it is a British carcase. Foreign meat has to be skinned to avoid the risk of importation of cattle-disease.

And, ultimately, that if you are about to drown yourself in the Thames, and are anxious to avert identification, the best spot to throw yourself off is in the neighbourhood of a ship at moorings, as then you are likely to be drawn under her and kept in the chains for months.

Some readers who are unaware that there were no gentlemen with coat-armour in the College of Apostles, may object that in presenting them to Wat I am introducing them to low society; but I can assure them that I have seen a very respectable Duke hail-fellow-well-met with a jockey, and my friend Wat has a far fuller education than the primest of jockeys. He is apt and accurate in quotations from English literature; and if you venture to make Greeks "meet" Greeks in his presence, or talk of fresh "fields" and pastures new, or attribute the tempering of the wind to the shorn lamb to Holy Writ, he will lay you ten to one in sovereigns you are wrong, and win your money. He is also a champion orthographist, and will back himself to spell English words against any man in the British Empire for £500, bar words technical.

"Ah," he said, "my noble! is it true you are going on a lecturing-tour next winter?"

"If God but spare me health and lung-power I am," was my reply.

"And wherefore, may I ask? Can you not do better at the desk?"

"The desk is monotonous; besides, I yearn for change, and I may be able to freshen up my ideas, and set down some notes in my tables. 'Twill improve intellectual and physical health."

"It will, of course," agreed Wat. "For instance, it will be perfectly delightful journeying to Inverness, say, in the depth of December."

"As it so happens, I am booked for Inverness on a date in that month."

Wat stared at me. "Do you know," he said, "'tis a far cry to Loch Awe, and Inverness is at the other side of Loch Awe? Thither and back from where we stand is eleven hundred and ninety miles."

I was surprised; I had not entered into these details; but I held my peace.

"Have you got many engagements?"

"Yes; the first was from Dollar, which I accept as a good omen; and, curiously enough, 'tis not in the United States."

"No," said Wat; "'tis between Edinburgh and Stirling. What fee do they tender you there?"

I told him.

"Ahem!" he continued, fondling his chin as he spoke. "If you don't cumber yourself with luggage—a courier-bag will do—and if you bus it to King's Cross, and stop at a temperance hotel in 'Auld Reekie,' and give servants no tips, and condescend to all invitations, with a wise economy, I take it, you won't drop more than five-and-twenty shillings on that transaction."

"How! What do you mean? You surely are not serious?"

"Why, the railway return fare to Edinburgh alone is five-pun-nine-and-six; and that will burn a hole in your fee."

"Perhaps," I ventured, not to look foolish, "I may have means of getting to Edinburgh for nothing."

"Ah!" said Wat, with a sigh and a sorrowful sententiousness, "if you think you can try on that, well and good; but I'm getting so precious fat that I can no longer hide myself under a seat!"

The barman, who had overheard the dialogue, here burst into an ill-bred fit of laughter. That attendant had some appreciation of humour; but Wat did the correct thing, nevertheless, in rebuking him for his untimely hilarity. The barman should have waited until he had retired to his own room.

This lecturing, as I explained to the financier, is rather a hazardous experiment after a man has passed his fortieth year. It is like learning to act— even more arduous than that, for you have no prompter, and must be qualified to think upon your legs. Interruptions must not check the flow of your eloquence; indifference must not chill your enthusiasm. You must be suave, alert, sonorous, and roll forth a discourse got off by rote as if it were the offspring of the moment's inspiration. The combustion of thought must appear to be a spontaneous combustion. Once your tale is set a-going, there must be no pause, no hesitancy; the electric current must be maintained to strong and constant power, or your audience sinks into a freezing dulness of courteous attention, which wishes, but fears, to yawn.

"Yes," said Wat, "the steam must be kept up. But if a Derby dog strays on the course—I mean if a bullock blunders on the track, what then?"

"That is the difficulty. It is vexatious if a man dozes off and endeavours to balance himself on the tip of his nose on the floor, when you are in the high ecstasy of a rhetorical period."

"I know," said Wat. "When you are what you call piling up the agony."

"Or when a deaf dowager is seized with a fancy to sternutate as you are waxing pathetic."

"Sternutate. That's a good word," remarked Wat admiringly. "I swear I could spell that. By-the-bye, how are you getting on with that book on Spain?"

Ecce iterum Crispinus.

"Good-afternoon I am just on my way home to write it."

*　　*　　*　　*　　*

The title I shall leave to the finish. Something catching is sure to suggest itself. The dedication I pencilled off months ago. Let that stand.

The subject, I think, is good. Spain is comparatively unknown. John Bull on his travels will not open to it. The British tourist in the Peninsula too often carries with him his native sense of superiority and his constitutional tendency to spleen. He turns up his nose at what he cannot, or will not, understand. If the beef is tough, he does not consider that it ought to be, most of the animals from whose ribs it came having done honest work as beasts of burden before they were driven to the slaughter-house. If the Val de Peñas is rasping to his palate, he ignores that the taste for wine, as for olives and Dublin stout and Glenlivat, is acquired. If the tobacco is coarse and weedy, he forgets that it is cheap, and that he can roll his cigarette and smoke it between the courses. But why does he not console himself for the absent by what is present—the ripe golden sun, the luscious fruits, the picturesque costumes, the high-bred dignity of the humblest beggar, the weird Æolian melody of sudden trills of song, the flashing eyes, mantilla-shaded, which speak romances in three volumes in every glance? The truth is, your Briton abroad, I mean the average one—not men like Mr. Gladstone in Sicily, or Captain Burton everywhere, Queen's Messengers and Special Correspondents, travelling Fellows of Oxford and pilgrims of art—your Briton of the tourist type is less inclined to adapt himself to another sphere than to try and assimilate that other to his own.

This tourist goes to Spain; he hurries from end to end of the Peninsula, his guide-book in his hand and his opera-glass across his shoulder; he pays a flying visit to the Escurial, and pronounces it a gloomy crib; drops in on Seville, sees it, and does not marvel; mayhap he wanders as far as Granada, and finds it a dreary "sell;" and then he returns homeward, hot and tired and disappointed, and is eloquent on the rapacity of innkeepers, the profusion of counterfeit coin, the discomforts and unpunctuality of locomotion, the shocking uncleanliness—but, however, "you know, we got on better than the Joneses; we saw more sights and covered more country in fewer days." And this peripatetic postures for the rest of his life as an authority on Spain! The only point, perhaps, on which his judgment is to be accepted is one which he might have learned in London, namely, that Price's circus is not quite so good as Sanger's in Westminster or Hengler's off Oxford Street. Out upon the poor fool! *He* know Spain! Why, that is more than I could dare to say, and I have had experience of it under Monarchy and Republic, in peace and in war; have mixed with Carlists in the field, and Intransigentes in the fortress; have traversed it from Irun to Gibraltar, from Santander to Malaga. He who has not been admitted into the intimacy of domestic life in Spain, who has not listened to habaneras by the camp-fire, joined in the jota on the village sward, shared in thorough sympathy in the sports of the arena and in the rites of religion, dipped into the peasant's olla podrida, nay, even watched the flushed gamblers over their cards, with the eager-eyed baratero standing by—he does not know Spain. All this have I done, and more; and yet I am but on the threshold of acquaintance with that great and beautiful home of paradox, that land of valour and courtesy, of fidelity and magnanimity, of piety and patriotism; and, in a lesser degree, of the vices which are opposed to these good qualities. No country of Europe so near to us is so little known. Yet in none is the soil fertilized by so much British blood. But this was in the bygone; and the yearly increasing swell of journeying-against-time tourists has not swept in tidal wave over the Peninsula. Even Spanish plays—and Spain can boast of one of the richest springs of dramatic literature in Europe—are comparatively sacred from the desecrating touch of the ruck of contemporary English stage adulterators.

Spain is not known; and yet it is not for the lack of word-painters to make it familiar in pen-and-ink pictures. There is Ford, most learned and graphic of guides, as full of irresistible prejudice as he is of impulsive affection. There is Borrow, that robust, quaint, and captivating, if sometimes over-fanciful, cicerone, albeit his errand to Spain was as indiscreet in purpose as it was bootless in result. There is Sala, of memory richly stored—whom I freely salute as past-master in his craft—most charming, observant, and illustrative of roving journalists. Ford, Borrow, Sala, all know Spain and "things Spanish" by personal experience; but it is plain that too many of the latter-day critics of Spain and the Spaniards are of the class who are ready to write social novels on Chinese life with no more knowledge of the Flowery Land than is to be obtained under the dome of the Reading-room of the British Museum. The pity of it is that this second-hand evidence is too often taken on trust, while the truthful records of eye-witnesses are shoved into a dusty corner of the cupboard. It is so nice to be patted on the head and rubbed down with the grain, to be reminded that we are what we always thought ourselves to be—the perfect, the registered A 1 people of the universe, the people who set the pattern, the people who are righteous, moral, honest, tolerant, charitable, and modest; who wage no unjust wars; who have no Divorce Court scandals; who know not bank frauds; who never persecuted Highlanders, or Jews, or Irishmen; who permit no misappropriations of money left to the poor; who make no brag over small victories against badly-armed savages. But stay, this is taking me to Africa, not Spain; and Africa does not begin at the other side of the Pyrenees, the epigram of Dumas to the contrary notwithstanding. My great object is to coax the English reader to be reasonable, and not to take the dimensions of the round world by the parochial yard-measure, nor to gauge the Coliseum by the standard of Clapham.

However, I shall not complete this work unless I make a start. *Dimidium facti*—but these odds and ends of Latin, which give to style an eighteen-penny polish of erudition and prove nothing, you can pick at will from "Swain's Collection of Easy Sentences." If I wait till I am in the mood, my suspense may be as long as that of the rustic on the bank of the stream. Perhaps Samuel Johnson, LL.D., was near the mark when he said that the author that thinks himself weather-bound will find, with a little help from hellebore, that he is only idle or exhausted.

And now a paragraph to elucidate why I have dedicated this book to a gentleman with whom I never exchanged a word. Apart from the bright and solid facts that he wards the weak, and has the pluck to change his opinions when he feels himself in the wrong, there are in his case two reasons all-sufficient to secure his counterfeit presentment a niche in my album, and himself a nook in my heart—he hath killed a bull in the arena, and he is husband of Byron's grand-daughter; and Byron was a poet—yea, a poet, I re-affirm, the hysterics to the contrary of sixteen screaming *laudatores Veneris* in non-lucid intervals counting for naught.

*   *   *   *   *

I have lost faith in Wat. In a moment of misplaced confidence I laid a wager on him at a spelling competition. He put one *n* in innuendo, and the *i* after the *ll*s in paillasse. If he had only gone to the root of the matter! I offered such long odds, too—a frayed copy of the "Iliad" to a gilt and morocco-bound set of the "Newgate Calendar."

CHAPTER II

The Old-Fashioned Invocation—"Them 'ere Spanish Kings!"—
Candidates for a Throne—*En Voyage*—Bordeaux and the Back-
ache—An Unmannerly Alsatian—The Patriot gets a Roland for his
Oliver—Small Change for a Hot Bath—Plan for Universal Coinage—
Daughters of Israel—The Jews Diagnosed—Across the Border—The
Writer is Saluted "Caballero"—Bugaboo Santa Cruz—Over a Brasero.

O MULES, liquorice, onions, oranges, garlic, and eke figs, cork and olives, and all you other products of Spain, come to my aid now that I enter upon my theme! Why should not a prose-chronicler of this era proffer his appeal as did the poets of era undetermined, of the eras of Augustus or the Second Charles? Perchance the $\Theta\varepsilon\alpha$, *Musa*, or Muse, to whom he makes his plea, may prove less kind than those to whom Homer, Virgil, or Milton prayed; but he has his remedy. In most instances, he can eat them.

Having complied with what used to be a hallowed custom, I shall now, following the example of that shrewd man, the late Abraham Lincoln, proceed to tell a story. The deadly sin in any book is dulness, and an occasional anecdote—if it point a moral so much the better—is sovran balsam for spleen.

I had a literary friend in London, and as he once returned to his residence by Regent's Park after a long walk, and asked had anyone called during his absence, the housekeeper replied "No;" but, correcting herself, added, "leastways, nobody, sir, except one of them 'ere Spanish kings!"

The Spanish king who was of no consequence was one of the race of Pretenders, and had the proud blood of countless generations of thick-lipped Bourbons meandering through his veins.

In the February of 1873, from which my personal knowledge of Spain dates, there were quite a number of these Spanish kings on the carpet. Amadeus, the Italian, had vacated the throne on the 11th, in a message which substantially affirmed that the peaceful government of Spain was hopeless—his Majesty gave it up as a bad job—and the two Chambers, combining as the sovereign Cortes, proclaimed the Republic by a majority of four to one. Of the aspirants to the crown there were notably Don Carlos Maria de los Dolores, the legitimate heir—if there be any virtue in legitimacy—and Don Alfonso, only son of the deposed Isabella, a boy of fifteen, at school at Vienna, a legitimate claimant if the abolition of the Salic law in 1830 be acknowledged. There was one who might have been a king, but sensibly declined the proffered honour, in the person of the ancient Espartero, Duke of Victory, Prince of Vergara; and there was a Prussian princeling, a

Hohenzollern-Sigmaringen, who had been nominated king in the midsummer of 1870, and whose nomination afforded the coveted pretext for the war between France and Germany. Besides, every Captain-General in the country—and the allowance is five—was a king *in prospectu*, not to mention the multifarious leaders of the many parties in the Congress, all of whom were qualified to be kings in their own conceit. Spain being thus suffering from a plethora of kings—as one result of which the Republic existed—it struck those who had commissioned me to chronicle the humours of besieged Paris that I might find some material for instructive and entertaining writing at the other side of the Pyrenees.

There are several ways of getting to Madrid. I had no difficulty in selecting mine—in fact, I had no choice. It was my duty to go there by the quickest route, no matter what the expense, the danger, or the inconvenience. These were the terms implied in my bond. The first stage was to Bordeaux. Over that I shall not dwell beyond a passing note on the excitement of the mad drive from terminus to terminus through Paris streets, in the early morn, at the rate of four statute miles an hour, in order, as Brother Jonathan has it, to "establish connection," and the misery of the long railway pilgrimage south. The scenery, I believe, was lovely; but fatigue, and the worry of a constrained position, and the frequent jerky stops as one was dozing to sleep, and the impatient summons "*en voiture*" as the hungry man was settling to a square meal, indisposed one for the proper appreciation of the picturesque. I got so eye-dazed from the whirl and dust and flitting sentinels of telegraph-posts on the long music-lines of telegraph-wires, that I could not distinguish a life-buoy from a funeral wreath. There were no sleeping-cars between Paris and Bordeaux then; back-ache, with an occasional variety in the shape of migraine, is my principal memory of that journey. Back-ache, the reader will allow, would take the poetry out of a honeymoon trip. And here I interpose a short parenthesis to register my acknowledgment to the philanthropist who invented sleeping-cars with their complementary accommodations. He is a benefactor to travelling humanity. Statues have been erected to dozens who have done less good to their kind—soldiers, lawyers, politicians, and patent pill-makers. Sleeping-cars avert exhaustion, ill-humour, bad dreams, and kidney-disease, not to exclude the back-ache and migraine afore-mentioned. Whenever a bronze memorial is to be raised on the Thames Embankment to their inventor, I am ready with my contribution.

At Bordeaux, where I shuffled into the nearest hotel, I uncoiled myself, and took the kinks out of my bones; but of the wine capital I shall say no more than that "I came, I slept, I left." At leaving, a little adventure variegated the itinerary. As I entered the railway-carriage, a gentleman on the opposite seat, its only occupant, was sucking an orange. I pulled out my cigar-case, and politely asked him if he had any objection to my smoking.

"Are you a German?" he demanded stiffly.

"Pardon me," I said, "I inquired if you had any objection to my smoking."

"Are you a German?" he repeated almost fiercely, his eyes flashing.

"I fail to see what business it is of yours what my nationality may be."

"It is my business, and I insist on your answering my question," he shouted, dropping the orange in his anger.

"And I decline to answer it," I said quietly.

Now he fairly raged. There is nothing which so provokes a man of hasty temper, with whom you may be in a controversy, as to preserve a tranquil, self-possessed demeanour. Ladies who nag their husbands are aware of this interesting feature in household ethics.

"Ah, you *are* a German!" he yelled. "You are a Prussian. I will not sit in the same compartment with you!" and he stood up, and danced, and went through a round of epileptic gesticulation.

"Your absence will not leave me inconsolable," said I, in soft, sweet accents, ceremoniously lifting my hat.

He bounced out of the carriage like a maniac, stamped along the platform, muttering with incoherent vehemence as he went, and presently reappeared with a gendarme, whom he informed that he suspected I was a Prussian spy. Interrogated, he could advance no proof beyond his own suspicions, my arrogant coolness of manner, and my hesitation in returning a straightforward reply.

"I am sure he is," he concluded, "for he all but admitted it."

The gendarme was perplexed, and asked me very civilly, was I a German?

"Distinctly not," I answered.

Had Monsieur any papers? I produced my British passport, which he looked at, pretended to understand, folded up, returned to me with excuses for having given me so much trouble, and fixed a look of grave reproach on his countryman. The latter was embarrassed, and had not the grace to make a frank apology, but mumbled something to the effect that I might have saved all this annoyance if I had stated what countryman I was at first.

"If you had put your question in the French fashion, that is to say courteously, I might have done so," I said.

He blushed, and stammered forth the apology at last; he hoped I would forgive his quickness, but he could not control himself when he met a German; he hated the race—the Germans were a pack of cold-blooded robbers, who had brought ruin on his country. He had vowed vengeance against them, and he had reason for it, for he was an Alsatian.

I saw my chance.

"*Mon Dieu!*" I exclaimed, throwing up my hands in affected horror. "It is you who are the German, then, and not I. Do you not know, sir, that Alsace has been a province of Germany for the past two years?"

If the face be an index to the mind, that Alsatian must have passed through a mental cyclone. Luckily for the angel who records bad language, his rage was so terrible that he lost the power of speech, the while I gently moved my head to and fro, and gazed at him with compassionate remonstrance, as much as to say how could he, a sausage-eating creature, have had the heart to pass himself off on me as a Frenchman? It was cruel, but it was merited. That Alsatian I despised as the meanest thing in patriotism I had ever met—and my experience of the article is not limited—for even were I a German, so long as I behaved myself with propriety he had no right to insult me by his surly cross-examination. But I suppose the poor devil thought he was playing the rôle of redresser of the wrongs of his country, and exacting an instalment of that *revanche* of which we hear occasional frothing babble. If I were a German I should be proud of it, and I hope I should have had the firmness to tell my Alsatian interlocutor so to his teeth.

From Bordeaux to Bayonne, down through the Landes, is a most interesting ride, as I dimly recollect; but I have no notes of it, and I infer that nothing particular occurred as I sped through the fat, nice, pleasant country. I had a short stay at Bayonne—long enough, however, to enable me to mark by ethnological signs and tinge of complexion that Spain was near. There were architectural signs, too, for there were colonnades in some of the streets to shelter promenaders from the powerful sun. Plenty of soldiers in Bayonne, and plenty of Hebrews. All of the latter seem to be engaged in the money-changing business. The whole art of money-changing consists in undervaluing the coin you are buying, and setting an exaggerated value on that you are giving for it. I must have lost a small fortune in the course of my money-changing transactions, therefore am I a most determined adherent of a uniform system of coinage for all civilized nations; and that coinage, I maintain, should be decimal. Fancy a foreigner getting small money for a sovereign after he has incurred a debt of one and sixpence for a hot salt-water bath on the South Coast! The fair attendant offers him a crown-piece, two half-crowns, two florins, two shillings, two six-pences, two groats, two threepenny bits, a postage stamp, a wheedling simper and a charity-bob. He is puzzled, and to my thinking he is justified in being puzzled; and if the attendant be not exceedingly attractive he is cheated. Coinage should be simple—should be so plain in identity that a child could distinguish it in the dark, and its worth should descend in regulated gradation. This reform will come eventually. One of the objections to a universal mintage may be that there would be a struggle as to whose profile should be sunk into the stamps—a point on which many rulers are solicitous, for they foresee that it is the only species of immortality they will ever attain. His Majesty of Araucania might legitimately protest against having his individuality merged in the lineaments of the artistic concretion of the Republic of San Marino, and the Queen of Madagascar (what is her name, by-the-bye?) might not easily be weaned from a natural longing for the luxury of having her own face in the perpetual youthfulness of Hebe imprinted on the discs which circulate at Tananarivo. That objection might be met in two ways; one side of the coin might be common to all the world, and the other reserved for the vanities, or the vanities might toss up, and acquire the renown of the numismatist's glass-case in turn.

That the reform will come I am convinced, but not while the Hebrews can hinder it. It is their interest to have this diversity of coinage; and they are very conservative of what is their interest. I have for a long time been trying to make up my mind about the Hebrews. My sympathies fly out to them because they have been persecuted, foully persecuted, on account of their religious belief, while, on the other hand, my antipathies are stirred because they make to themselves an idol of gold. Beautiful are the daughters of Israel with a striking Old Testament beauty, marvellously imperious considering the lengthened apprenticeship of helotry through which they have served; but *naïveté* is not the quality one would look for in their countenances. As well seek a dimple, or a blush, or a coy reserve. Oh! beautiful indeed, and to an imposing degree, with long straight nose, full orbs, pursing lips, clean-chiselled regular contour; but the earliest lesson they learn is how many grains Troy go to a silver shekel. They may have in them still the fire of Jael, who drove the tent-peg into the skull of the tyrant, or the fierce genius of the poetic Deborah, who was one of the first to strike the lyre of triumph; but, alas! that it must be said, the gentle Ruth, gleaning in the fields of barley, is a lost tradition of the race. I can almost imagine the tender-eyed Leah and the well-favoured Rachel figuring in an idyl of another Wakefield family; but, then, where are we to seek for them? Not in Bayonne. There are no artless Jewesses there; the pupils under their black lashes glitter with the glow of cupidity, and I prefer the light of love. There is something in it more womanly and mellow. I have seen the eyes of a Jewess almost bulge out of their sockets like those of the telescope fish, as she gazed on the treasures of Notre Dame at Paris—to me a degrading dilatation—and I set it down to the instincts engendered by centuries of servitude, when the Jews discovered that the surest mode of checkmating their masters was by amassing money, and lending it out to them at usurious rates. Certes, they are a pushing and clannish tribe, and skilled in the mimetic arts; but they are not so high-souled and all-influential as their friend Disraeli would fain make them in a chapter of elaborate gush in that fine novel, "Coningsby." In the main I admire them; but I could wish that they stripped to manual toil oftener; that they were less obsequious in indigence, and less despotic and dictatorial when they are in authority—niggers and Hindoos can be that; that they were less prone to exhibit their entire stock-in-trade in the shop-window; that they were less ostentatious in their hospitality, when they are hospitable, and that they had a quieter taste in raiment. Now, I think I have had ample retribution out of that greasy matron at Bayonne, who exploited me when converting my honest notes of the Bank of England into Spanish duros.

From Bayonne the train rattled along not far from the fringe of the Bay of Biscay, by Biarritz and St. Jean de Luz, and across the bridge spanning the Bidassoa to Irun, the border town of Spain, close by Fontarabia's wooded height. Here we had a pause for customs and passport examination and change of carriages. No railway official could give me any information as to how far the line went; it might go to Madrid, it might not go more than a few miles; the country was unsettled. These officials impressed me as sulky or stupid or timorous, or all three combined, and made glaring contrast with the smart servants on the London, Chatham and Dover line, who know everything that regards their calling, and are always quick and decisive in answer without taint of rudeness. But I was recalled from my comparisons by one word, which wrought a magic effect upon me.

That word was "*caballero!*"

How elated I felt! I realized that I was in Spain, and seemed to grow in inches and self-esteem. I lent myself to an unconscious swagger, tipped my hat jauntily on one side of my head, and was swayed by an almost irresistible inclination to retire to some unobserved corner and wax the ends of my moustache.

The speaker was a Guardia Civil, the Spanish equivalent for a French gendarme. A solemn man in a cocked-hat, protected by a glazed cover, his complexion was of sickly walnut-juice sallow, like the flesh-tint on a portrait in oils by an old master. The complexion was characteristically Spanish. He was the State personified, and had much dignity. He told me I might count upon getting to Beasain, a village in a valley at this side of one of the mountains of the Pyrenean range, but that progress beyond that by rail was problematical, as the Cura Santa Cruz had torn up the track.

This was the first I had heard of the Cura Santa Cruz, one of the most ferocious and redoubtable of the partisans of Don Carlos. Truculent were the stories which were told of him. He was Raw-head-and-bloody-bones in cassock; priest and picaroon, with a well-developed tendency towards wholesale murder; Bogie with a breviary—that is, according to some.

- 16 -

According to others, he was a brave, disinterested and reverend patriot; a sort of Hofer-cum-Tell individual, etherealized by the sanctity of his vocation. Anyhow, be he maleficent or benign, it was clear that he was Somebody, and had filled the whole country-side with awe. He led a corps of guerrilleros, who rejoiced in the nickname of the Black Band; and such was the terror inspired by their exploits, that the whisper that Santa Cruz was hovering near stunned opposition, and brought in any ransom demanded. He must have been in one of his benign moods on this occasion, for he permitted our train free passage through his territory; and in the evening we drew up in a snow-bound basin, where shuddered the straggling hamlet of Beasain. I took up my lodging for the night in a two-storied cabin, and sent a news-letter to London, recounting what I had seen and heard so far. I was urged to this by an intimation which had reached me, that a rival had preceded me on the road to Madrid by twenty-four hours. The first blow is half the battle, and I calculated that if I could get the ear of the public in advance of him, there would be a point gained. Communication with England was open from Beasain. Heaven knows how it would be to-morrow or next day.

There was fearful tangible evidence of the presence of Santa Cruz in this remote valley. At one extremity where the cavernous opening of the railway tunnel made a dark gap in the hillside, the track had been wrenched from its fastenings, and the sleepers smeared with oil and set on fire. Heaps of charred timber marked the spot, and alongside, down in a ravine, lay the wreck of shattered carriages and locomotive, just as they had been tumbled in a topsy-turvy blending of complete collapse. It made me tremble to reflect what this meant, and I came to the conclusion that Santa Cruz was thoroughgoing in his warfare and restrained by few scruples of compassion.

Over the fumes of the brasero, the brass-pan with its stifling embers of charcoal, placed on a stand in the middle of my room, my landlord and I with outstretched palms held long confab before I turned into bed. His mother had been French, and we gossiped in that tongue. His views were tolerably impartial, but it was plain that the Carlists had his good wishes. The factions were partially dispersed, but were not defeated, he said; they would give more trouble; and then he horrified me with a well-authenticated tale of a recent fight at Aspeitia, where an old villager had taken refuge in a house which was subsequently occupied by the troops. He fell dead after a volley fired by the Carlists. His son was one of those who had joined in the volley, and the awful muffled rumour was spreading among the peasantry that it was by the son's bullet the father had been slain.

CHAPTER III.

A Make-Believe Spain—The Mountain Convoy—A Tough Road to Travel—Spanish Superiority in Blasphemy—Short Essay on Oaths—The Basque Peasants—Carlism under a Cloak—How Guerilla-Fighting is Conducted—A Hyperborean Landscape—A Mysterious Grandee—An Adventurous Frenchman—The Shebeen on the Summit—Armed Alsasua—Base Coin.

AND this is sunny Spain, the land of the olive and the vine. Spain it certainly is in the absolute sense of the word in political geography, but in no other. It is no more Spain than the Highlands are England. The language, the race, the habits, the growths, are different. The language, the Euscara, is known to only one man not born within the borders, the polyglot Prince Lucien Buonaparte. A hackneyed legend runs that the devil tried to learn it, and dislocated his jaw. The race is the aboriginal Iberian, and has none of the languor of the south in it—a stubborn, not a supple race. The habits of the people are industrious. The growths are rather of the apple and the pine than the olive and the vine.

There before us rises the wall of Nature's handiwork which shuts us out from the true Spain.

In my boyhood I often gazed with admiration on a print of Napoleon crossing the Alps. He was astride of a prancing white charger. I have since learned to detest Napoleon, and to know more of mountain travel. That masterful general, but cruel, dishonourable, bad man—demon-man with genius undoubted and will unbendable, but with the most unscrupulous of insatiate and insensate ambitions, and a leaven of littleness—did not face the heights of St. Bernard on a mettlesome steed, but on a patient mule, and the luxury of his apparel was restricted to furs. Wrapped up in the thickest clothing I could find, I watched the convoy forming outside the station at Beasain in the sunlit cold.

The train from San Sebastian got in at nine in the morning, and before ten a procession of six waggons, built after the massive, clumsy fashion of the French diligence, was drawn up in line. Horses and mules, generally in teams of five—three leaders and two wheelers—were yoked to the ramshackle vehicles. The passengers, muffled in cloaks, rugs, scarfs, shawls and comforters—for there was ice in the breath of the keen air of the mountain—literally packed themselves in the narrow "insides" of the old-fashioned coaches. There were five in the low, narrow hutch upon wheels with myself, all males; we were as close as sardines in a box. There were some ladies of the party. I trust they had more space at their disposal. The luggage was piled on the roofs and covered with tarpaulins, the drivers mounted the seats in front, whips were cracked, and off we bounded at a pace that would rouse the applause, or peradventure the envy, of the gentlemen who tool the Brighton coach. Gaily our skinny steeds breasted the rise, sending a curl of mist from their hides, and shaking merry music out of the collars of bells round their necks as they clattered over the hard road. For three miles we dashed along at express speed. How spirit-stirring is rapid motion! I actually was warming into a wild joy, and praying that we might encounter the Carlists, under the influence of this gallop in the bracing morning atmosphere.

Suddenly there is a stop. The Carlists? No. But here the ascent begins, and a body of mountaineers await us with a string of bullocks. The three leaders are unharnessed and attached behind; and eight bullocks, two by two, are yoked in front of the pair of mules who act as wheelers. The same is done with the other waggons. I watch this process of yoking the bullocks with much curiosity. A strong piece of board is run across the heads of the pair who are coupled, and firmly tied in front of the horns; a sheepskin is thrown over that, for what purpose I cannot tell; and the ropes by which the bullocks drag us are fastened to the piece of board afore-mentioned. They pull, not against the shoulder, but against the horn. Their owners, muscular peasants, lightly clad, though it is cold, walk beside them with long pointed sticks, and occasionally goad them in the flanks. When that does not suffice, they push them, or rain blows on their hides, or twist their tails, and when all other means fail they swear at them. But the grave oxen move no quicker; they cling to their own gait as if deeply convinced of the truth of the adage, "Fair and easy goes far in the day." The peasants call one "demonio" and another a cow; but the sleepy pair keep never minding, as they waddle along with drooping heads, held closely together as if whispering conspiracy.

At this early point in my experiences, the painful knowledge is forced upon me that the Spaniards are highly accomplished in the art of imprecation. If our army swore terribly in Flanders, I have my theory to account for it. They must have picked up the habit there, and the Spaniards under Alva had left their traces behind them in the speech of the region they had occupied. As a rule, swearing betrays a poverty of invention; it is the resource of the vulgar and ignorant to emphasize their assertions; but in Spain the swearing developed an originality that almost reconciled one to it. There was an awful insolence, a ribald riotousness in some of the oaths which redeemed them from the scorn which every well-balanced mind should feel for displays of petulance. I respect a good round oath—an oath that blanches my cheeks and makes me imagine that it would not be extraordinary if the ground were to open and swallow the varlet who uttered it. That sort of oath is to be tolerated for its audacity. The malediction is a higher form of oath, and some maledictions are magnificent. To the amateur I can recommend King Lear's upon Cordelia, Francesco Cenci's upon Beatrice—which is more Shakspearian than Shakspeare—and even puny Moore's upon the traitorous Gheber. The joint-stock oath which Sterne puts into the mouths of the Abbess of Andoüillets and the novice, Margarita, who had the whitlow on her middle finger, is passable for its fantastic ingenuity; and the strong locutions pat in the lips of a certain Duke—unless notoriety belies him—are to be licensed because of his rank, and because he is a soldier. But he should have the courage to blurt them out on all occasions. He who dares to outrage society should not shrink from offending an individual.

"You —— naughty boy, why did you sound the wrong call?" said H.R.H. to a bugler, but as soon as he got out of earshot of a certain Personage, he muttered in an angry undertone, "You canonized little beggar, you know what I meant."

The Spaniards are liberal and earnest and dogged in their railings, anathemas, and execrations, but still the sleepy oxen do not hurry themselves. They care no more for a volley of select comminations than the jackdaw of Rheims did for the archbishop's curse. Of a verity this bullock's pace is a snail's pace, and we have ample leisure to inspect the peasants as we crawl along. Brawny, hardy, and firmly-knit as Highlandmen, their faces are weather-beaten and frank; their manner, when one speaks to them, independent but polite; in dress like unto their Celtic kinsmen of Brittany, short-jacketed, loose, and slovenly, but in stature more like to the tall mountaineers of Tipperary. They must be poor, very poor; but they have the appearance of content, and with it of honesty, sobriety, and civility.

And now a little secret must be imparted. Every man-jack of these ox-drivers is a Carlist, and that is the reason we are not attacked to-day! In a week those innocent clowns may be blazing away at the regular army of Spain from the brushwood on a hillside, for after such fashion are Carlist wars conducted. A band assembles at the call of some chief—that is to say, the peasants leave their cabins and meet at some rock, some conspicuous tree, or some cross-roads. They have with them a flag, perhaps; perhaps a priest or two; they are badly armed with such arms as insurgents carry—blunderbusses, flint-muskets, fowling-pieces, horse-pistols; they have no distinctive uniform, except a few of the older bands—the permanent army of Carlism—which are clad in the seedy clothes that the French Garde Mobile wore during the late war. The campaign opens; a descent is made upon some village, the mayor is asked to supply so many hundred rations, and the young men are summoned to join the flag. Sometimes the mayor refuses, and there is a fight between "the volunteers of liberty," that is to say, the local national guard, and the Carlists. On the average, so the reports go, one man is killed in each of these combats, and three wounded. That is a battle at this stage of the Carlist war. With the regular troops sent against them the Carlists act otherwise. They take up ground in some inaccessible eyrie, pop at the passing detachments from their ambuscade, draw them on in the hope of catching them in a trap; but the troops are cautious, they pepper away at the Carlists from a distance until the Carlists run, and the affair ends, as usual, with the loss of one man killed and three wounded. The peasants return to their cabins to tell the tale of their gallantry, and if the troops perchance should come their way, why they are but inoffensive, ingenuous tillers of the soil, the most peaceful beings on the face of nature. The firearm is hid in the thatch or in the neighbouring hedge. But the officers who lead the troops do not allow their enemies the monopoly of gasconade. In the *Gaceta de Madrid* the bulletin of the engagement duly appears, and the names of the doughty warriors are chronicled for the admiration of the señoritas. One Carlist chief—at least, so pretend the wags—had been killed outright thrice, wounded mortally five times, and has had his band completely dispersed and broken up seven times in the *Gaceta*, and yet he is still alive and troublesome. A most outlandish war, but how disastrous in its effects on the trade and prosperity of the country! It could not be carried on if the soil were not rich to plenteousness. There is an adventurous vigour in the breed, too, and the terrain lends itself to guerilla fighting. So far, I know nothing of the merits of Carlism; but this I can divine, that it is the old rivalry betwixt town and country, and the "pagans" or villagers are all Carlists—question of transmitted feud or local traditions, or both. The rustics have the advantage over the town-bred men; they are familiar with the by-paths; every sheiling is a refuge for them, every dweller therein a self-constituted scout. When they choose to seek them, they must have secure hiding-places. Artillery is an arm of derision in the hills; cavalry can rarely act effectually, and in the way of reconnoitring is next to useless, as its movements can be espied from rock-cover on every eminence; but in the open these insurgents can do nothing against disciplined troops. Pity that they should be such fools as to abandon their pleasant and comfortable, if humble, homesteads, to help on the aspirations of any right-divine make-believe claimant to the heaven-sent mission—by accident of birth—of impressing other human beings that he is wiser than they, and should have revenues and reverence for condescending to govern them.

What would our ox-drivers do, I wonder, if they could overhear and understand the conversation in which thoughts like these are exchanged in the lumbering Noah's ark they are helping through their domain? We are getting nigh and nigher to the clouds, and the quilt of snow on the mountain grows thicker. The pathway is traceable only by the marks of the hoofs of beasts of burden and the ruts of wheels, and the fleecy banks at each side rise gradually higher. It is palpably colder, and yet we are far from the culminating point of the Pyrenean pass; straight saplings are not infrequent around, and here and there a lowly hut in a nook under some sheltering rock, both hut and rock hoary with snow, startles us with the reminder that human beings actually live here. The Basques, said Voltaire, are a people who sing and dance on the summit of the Pyrenees. Our ox-drivers do not sing, neither do our muleteers. This interminable glare is becoming very fatiguing to the eyes, and the higher we ascend the rarer are the refreshing little streaks of darker hue. Stumps of dwarf trees replace the straight saplings to be seen lower down; and hardly are we on the crest of one snow-capped hill than another, hidden under the same smooth sheet of everlasting lime-white, mocks us. Slowly and painfully the oxen toil along, and the peasants by their side sink knee-deep at every step. Will this ever end? It was picturesque at first to watch the long caravan coiling over the spiral track which turns right and left like a corkscrew. Now it is tedious, for we are chilled and worn-out, hungry and cramped. The sublimity of nature is grandiose, but there may be too much of it. One tires of rolling perpetual cigarettes; one even tires of studying the forcible Spanish adjurations that begin with the third letter of the alphabet. My companions, four French commercial travellers, relapse into silence and doze off into fitful starts of the sleepiness begot of extreme cold; the fifth— a grandee of Castile I take him to be at the very least by his appearance, broad swarthy countenance, shaven upper lip and chin, and short spade whiskers of a night-black—the fifth, this Spaniard, did not relapse into silence, for he had never uttered a word since we started.

What weariness to the flesh is this tedious climb to regions hyperborean! I catch myself yawning. What if our waggon were to break down! At last one of the Frenchmen bursts out, "*Dieu de Dieu, j'en ai assez.*" He would stand or rather sit it no longer, opened the door, and alighted. We all followed his example, even to the taciturn Spaniard, and took to the road. A walk in advance might send the blood circulating, and on we plodded in the middle of the path, regardless of the snow which soaked into our boots and saturated our trousers to the knees. Not a living being was visible but two crows who bore us company, and hopped on our flanks like a covering-party. The road was tantalizing in its tortuousness; after walking a furlong we found ourselves a couple of yards directly above the point we had quitted a quarter of an hour before. One of the Frenchmen, seeing this, had an inspiration; he determined to go up the mountain perpendicularly, and before we could dissuade him he had sunk to his armpits in a treacherous crevasse. We dragged him out by making a cable of our pocket-handkerchiefs and throwing it to him. He took his wetting in good part.

"Ah!" he cried, "shan't I have something to tell them when I get back to the Boulevard des Italiens." And then, as if reflecting, he added, "But no, 'twill never do; they'd call me *farceur*."

A red-brick building with an arrangement of iron on the roof, as if it had been employed as a signal-post, faced us—high up on the pinnacle of a ridge at one moment; was at our side the next; behind us anon; and directly before us now. By turns it was small and large. We were asking ourselves (all except the Spaniard; he never spoke) was this a phantasmagoria, when a jingle of bells was heard on the still air. Where did it come from? We could see nothing. Suddenly, as a theatrical ghost springs from a trap-door, at an abrupt turn a wild figure appears bearing right down upon us. A Carlist chieftain? Not so fast. A muleteer simply, sitting sideways on his prad, and leading a half-dozen mules laden with panniers in Indian file behind him. He told us we had reached the summit, and that there was a fonda a short distance off. Signs of life multiplied; we met mountaineers, with oxen drawing small cars with solid wheels similar to those of toy carriages—wheels that kept up perpetual creak and croak—and finally we encountered the caravan from Alsasua to Beasain. But we encountered no Carlists, that is, no armed Carlists, for every man there is Carlist in soul. The smoky fonda was as miserable as the most miserable of Irish shebeens; yet they gave us good white bread and eggs to eat, and, with the aid of the sauce of hunger and sundry glasses of acid Val de Peñas to wash it down, we made a hearty meal. The caravan overtook us in half an hour; the rest of the journey was downhill, the snow was deeper than on the other side, and the jolting terrific, but we did not care. Our goal was near, and we had eaten and drunk. We laughed at the dangers we had passed, and even the Spaniard unbent and exhibited unexpected powers of conversation. Alas! for my judgment; he was no grandee of Castile, but a butcher from Saragossa, a mere *carnifex* with blood of the common red tint.

At Alsasua we came upon a village bleaker than Beasain, with soldiers billeted under every roof. They loitered in twos and threes about the wide street, which was drab with patches of dirty snow. Here were placed a few mountain guns under custody of a shivering sentry, there a bugler in slovenly greatcoat blew some call with pinched lips on a battered instrument. At the station—a rude shanty with wooden partitions and a plank erection run up as refreshment-stall—some attempt had been made at fortification. There were mud-works thrown up in its vicinity, and the walls were roughly loop-holed. A party of Linesmen were in possession. On a siding close by was the locomotive which had been riddled with shot by the insurgents on the now disused line to Pampeluna. Our own locomotive was awaiting us, with steam up, and I hurried to procure my ticket. I pushed a piece of honest red gold through the wicket, and an extremely nice, slim female clerk gave me the pasteboard with my change and thanks. Something struck me in the silver shoved towards me; the leaden hue of the pesetas was suspicious. I took up one and rung it; the dull sound convinced me it was bad. I rung another— same result. I was desolate; but I had to call the attention of the extremely nice girl to the error she had fallen into; and she coolly, without adumbration of a blush, or faintest pretence at apology, took back the base coins, and gave me their equivalent in coins that were sterling. And then, for the first time, it broke upon me, that it was not considered a scoundrelly act to pass bad money upon an innocent foreigner, or upon an innocent native, for the matter of that. I further learned that if I had removed that bad money from the counter, I should have had to bear with the loss. That extremely nice girl would have assured me with all politeness that I must be labouring under an illusion.

The Spaniard has personal dignity to a prodigious degree. But his personal dignity does not hinder the ordinary Spaniard from endeavouring to foist counterfeit stamps upon his neighbour whenever he has the chance.

The tarantara of a bugle stirred a company of soldiers to take their places in the train. They were our escort to Miranda, on the borders of Old Castile, where we might consider ourselves out of danger. It is my opinion we were never in any danger.

We reached Miranda safely, and from that swept down in the darkness to Madrid without molest, the most of us snoring as regularly as the funnel of the engine snorted. I had a fearsome vision of a sweet Spanish maiden who had knowingly placed a worthless peseta in the tirelire at Mass, and had been sentenced by Santa Cruz to grill on the gridiron of hell for the term of her natural life. A carpet-bag utilized as a pillow was the origin of my vision. Had that carpet-bag been more carelessly packed, the penalty on the poor girl might have been prolonged to eternity.

CHAPTER IV.

Madrid—The Fonda and its Porter—The Puerta del Sol—Postal Irregularities—Tribute to the Madrileños—The Barber's Pronunciamiento—Anecdotes of King Amadeus—Checkmating the Grand Dames—Queen Isabella—The Embarrassed Mr. Layard of Nineveh—The Great Powers Hesitate—America Goes Ahead—General Sickles—Mahomet and the Mountain—Republicanism among the troops—A Peculiar Pennsylvanian Dentist—Castelar under Torture—The Writer meets one of his Sept—Politicians by Trade—Honour among Insurgents—Alonso the Reckless.

FIRST impressions of Madrid, "the only court," do not fill the visitor with awe. It is an aggregate of masonry, fragmentary on the edges, compact in the middle, on a sandy plateau in a waste of arid landscape. There is lack of natural shade and water, albeit there are tree-planted walks and gardens, with cedars and Himalayan pines, and fountains with fulness of clear flow are abundant. It wants a river; the Manzanares, I am told, is but a ditch. I do not know if that is so; I never could see the Manzanares. A rugged, sun-blistered city, Madrid struck me as no more characteristically Spanish—or what I had taught myself to accept as such—than Turin is Italian; both are half-Frenchified. In the northern distance are the summits of the Guadarrama hills, and the unseen breeze which sweeps down from its snowy eyries amongst them cuts like an icicle. The Madrileño fears it, for it has a trick of permeating the streets with a subtile, chilling, killing breath; and when the Madrileño steps from the sunny to the shady side of the street he is careful to lift a corner of his cloak as screen to his mouth.

The central point of Madrid is the Puerta del Sol—a bare, broad, irregular area off which nine thoroughfares diverge. Round it the day-god, greatest friend of Spain, pivots in glory. Now he floods one side with radiance, now he drops his cloth of gold over another. The Puerta del Sol is the focus of interest for the population. Thither the gossips repair, and there the affairs of the nation are discussed very often by those who have acted, act, or hope to act as leaders of the nation. Naturally I made for the Puerta del Sol, for it was of vital importance to me to be in the movement, in the very vortex of the pool. I was fortunate. I got rooms in the Fonda de Paris, an hotel at the corner of the Calle de Alcalá, the principal avenue leading from the Plaza. As proof of the unsettled condition of affairs and its effect upon trade, it need only be said that at the *table d'hôte* of this, the first hotel in the capital, where one hundred and thirty persons usually sit down to dinner, there were sometimes not more than fifteen or twenty, and a proportion of these were fly-about Special Correspondents. Yet in this exiguous circle of prudent people who were detained in Madrid, or foolhardy people who had travelled there, turned up the irrepressible British tourist. Of the latter class we had charming specimens at dinner one evening in two English girls, with fresh peachy complexions, and hair like wavy masses of ripe maize. They had no guide but their faithful "Murray." What became of them subsequently I never ascertained; but it is to be trusted they were as lucky as the enterprising young lady who relied on Erin's honour and Erin's pride in the reign of King Brian, and made the tour of the Emerald Isle with a gold ring on the tip of a wand. That would hardly pay the hotel-bills nowadays.

A great feature in the fonda was Constantine, the hall-porter, a tall swarthy man, who was as fluent a linguist as an Alexandria dragoman. He was Greek by birth, but had a strain of English blood on the mother's side. His sire may have been a South Sea cannibal or a South African lion-slayer for aught I remember; but that there was something phenomenally bold in him I am certain. Constantine's instincts were predatory, and his manners morose. There was a tradition that he had been a bandit in the neighbourhood of Smyrna, or an innkeeper by the Marseilles docks—much about the same thing, and that he was prepared to do little jobs of human carving for a consideration. However, these may have been fables got up by travellers in search of excitement to invest Constantine with an interesting air of romance. He was very civil to me and did not cheat me more than I chose. I never had occasion to ask him to kill anybody.

From my windows I could command the mid-basin in the Plaza, more for use than ornament, and as great a rendezvous of the quidnuncs as a village-pump. The panorama of life lounged or moved or bustled beneath—shifting groups of cloaked disputants, veiled women tripping gracefully along, stately Civil Guards in three-cornered hats, sombre priests with Don Basilio head-gear, the various moulds of human nature from the grandee to the mendicant, and above all that brood with which I soon grew familiar, and for which I conceived an invincible disgust—the sallow, peering, prating, importunate brood of hungry place-hunters, impatient to dip their fingers into the Government pie. Cabriolets passed to and fro, tram-cars with such sleek well-conditioned mule-teams jolted on the rails; here a horse-soldier trotted by with clattering accoutrements, there a water-carrier sturdily trudged; and in a sheltered angle a long-locked vendor of a magic hair-restorer vaunted his wondrous balm in sonorous patter, and occasionally curtained his face with his thick mane brought over from his back as tangible testimony to the fertilizing properties of the balm. In short, from those windows I could take in the cardiac pulsing of Madrid. Below me, as I sat and smoked my cigarette, the beginning of change or crux, accident or riot, the initial whims or humours of the populace, the formation of a procession or the overture of a pronunciamiento, were within my ken. And at one corner of the Puerta were the General Post Office and Telegraphic Bureau, a matter of great convenience to me, if only they were properly managed. However, it was far easier to collect news than to send it to the desired destination. The post was as unsafe as in those days in another land when Mr. Richard Turpin, highwayman, and his comrogues intercepted his Majesty's mails. As for messages by wire, I was not long in learning that no important information was allowed to be sent; true, the money for its transmission was taken, but—delayed, or forwarded, or suppressed even—the strict rule in that establishment was "no money returned." Vain were complaints. The Special Correspondent had no resource but that of the negro suffering from toothache; 'twas his to grin and bear it. The idea of ever again seeing the colour of the coin which has passed into the palm of a Spanish functionary is laughable in its pastoral innocence. As well expect to handle last year's snow. The system of ignorant espionage still obtained in the Peninsula, as I was forced reluctantly to observe: the word "Cuba" or "Carlos" on the telegraphic form at once aroused the scruples and suspicions of the official, and led to the confiscation of the message. In the end, I discovered how to facilitate the despatch of news; but as that is my secret I keep it to myself. Suffice it that in my bill of expenses the item "sundries" was elastic.

There are some valuable guide-books to Spain, and to them I refer the reader if he desire to be crammed with curious knowledge about churches and picture-galleries, museums of arms, and the beautiful upholstery of the Duke of Sixty-Blazons' palace. My behest was with living not dead Spain, as investigated during the throes of a political convulsion. I made my notes on the Madrileños without bias, and without bias I give them. I spent five weeks in constant and free intercourse with all classes of the inhabitants. During that time I did not detect one Belleville face; I did not catch the glitter of a knife except at a dinner-table, nor remark a single drunkard staggering along the streets. Yet I was in every quarter of the town, to the lowest, at all hours. There are parts of London where the foreign visitor could not penetrate and come back with the same story. The Madrileños are indolent—granted; but they are frugal, temperate, and well-conducted. Occasionally a poniard is slipped into the ribs of an enemy, but mistakes will occur in the best-regulated families. If this be a vindictive and blood-sucking people, the vampirism is adroitly concealed; the dirty linen must be washed in the dark corner where the charcoal is stored, so that Paul Pry may not be gratified with the sight. There is no working population at Madrid; there are no large manufactories, no thriving centres of employment. That is one reason why Madrid is orderly compared to other and livelier cities. Prosperous Barcelona swarms with mechanics and artisans, and that is one reason why Barcelona is disorderly. The rights-of-man agitators generally find favour there. The International has its ramifications in the Catalonian capital. In Madrid, the International is a pigmy failure. Its emissaries came once and laboured zealously to stir up the son of toil to a proper consciousness of his dignity. After months of propagandism they succeeded in persuading Figaro to shake a rebellious pole and fiercely flourish his lathering-brush.

"Know, ye smooth-lipped minions of the despot Capital," quoth the barbers in an indignant round-robin, "we shall no longer submit to the gross tyranny of shaving you before eight of the morning!"

But Figaro was defeated; Madrid let its beard grow.

The sudden departure of the Italian-bred monarch had apparently plunged the politicians into a pit of bewilderment. They did not know how they stood. Amadeus after his reign of five-and-twenty months had perchance left few partisans behind him, but assuredly no enemies. His principal fault, but that was fatal, consisted in his being a foreigner. It was universally vouchsafed that he was very brave, a true hidalgo in that respect, and if he had been removed in the orthodox method by revolution or the assassin, his name would have been garlanded with rosemary for remembrance. But Spanish pride was nettled to the quick at the cavalier way he had tossed back, with a shrug of the shoulders, the gift of a crown when he had tired of it. He had looked upon the throne of Castile as a gewgaw to be surrendered with indifference, and steamed contentedly to Italy to enjoy his comparatively obscure Dukedom and rank of General in preference. He had chosen the wiser and happier part, but to those he had abandoned it was mortifying in the extreme. Still, he was an unquailing chevalier, almost fit to be a Spaniard, this son of Victor Emmanuel. He had disarmed hostility, and compelled the praise of the envious, the very day he entered Madrid, forty-eight hours after the funeral of Prim, when he spurred ahead of his escort and offered his breast undismayed to the aim of any or all assassins.

That entry of Amadeus could not have inspired him with much of the buoyancy of a bright expectation. There was in it more of sanguinary suggestiveness than sanguine hope. The ghostly presence at the King's first dinner in the palace could not be denied—that of the slaughtered "Paladino," no longer fiery and strenuous, but a figure, inert, waxen, blood-bolstered, a bullet-riddled flesh-target It was most unpropitious of entries. There was an odour of cerecloth in the tapestry, the yellow hue of immortelles in the épergnes, a sediment of bitterness in the wine-cup, a strain of melancholy in the music. And yet there was some semblance of gaiety, for with all his austere stateliness your Spaniard is very like unto the Irishman:

"With one auspicious, and one dropping eye,

With mirth in funeral, and with dirge in marriage,

In equal scale weighing delight and dole."

There were sundry plots to take the life of Amadeus, but Providence protected him, and he made it a point, after each attempt or threat, to show himself in public with the ostentation of a reckless courage. He rode or walked about with a single aide-de-camp, which was a crime with those monarchists who set store by the pageantry of state. On one occasion, as he was returning to the palace, the horse in a hackney-coach with a fat bourgeois inside took fright, and started off at break-neck speed, overtaking the King's carriage. The King's coachman whipped up his team, but the wheels of the two vehicles had locked in each other, and the horses galloped frantically side by side. The aide-de-camp, fearing a new and daring experiment in regicide, snatched his rapier from the sheath and began furiously prodding through the window of the hackney-coach. The fat bourgeois shrunk and flattened himself into a corner, drew in his breath, and dodged the lunges of the searching steel. When the palace-gates were reached, and the animals were stopped, the unfortunate citizen was extricated from his hazardous position more dead than alive. He was glistening with the wetness of fright, trembled like an aspen, and blubbered as he begged for mercy. The panelling was pierced, and the cushion ripped into rags; but by some extraordinary luck the poor man, who was a harmless dealer in provisions, had escaped without a scratch. But he owned that he never before had five minutes of such violent exercise complicated with vile terror. During the scene Amadeus kept his seat tranquilly, and relaxed into a smile as he discovered the mistake of his too-zealous companion.

The conspiracies of the saloons were more successful, as efforts to annoy without contravening law always are. They are not so readily met. And the malicious ingenuity of woman, when she lays herself out to be offensive, is remarkably inventive and diabolically persistent. Some of the grand dames of Madrid had the impish inspiration to put the Royal couple into Coventry. There is a fashionable carriage-drive in the capital corresponding much to ours between Hyde Park Corner and Queen's Gate. Whenever Amadeus and his spouse went there for an airing, the blue-blooded of the opposition significantly trotted off. Once an immense procession of the aristocratic families made its appearance, and slowly and perseveringly "took the dust." Such a turn-out of gala equipages had not been witnessed for years. All the ladies were arrayed in the ancient Spanish costume; the fan and veil with high comb and carnation in the hair in every case replaced the Parisian bonnet and parasol. It was a protest against the foreign dynasty, and was clearly meant as a demonstration of insult. One of the Royal household was equal to the provocation; whether Spaniard or Italian I am not sure, but the latter I think, so subtle was his revenge. He went round to all the houses of ill-fame in the capital that night, and entered into conversation, burnished with duros, with their female occupants. The next evening Madrid was afforded the spectacle in its most fashionable drive of a parade of courtesans, in ancient Spanish costumes, fanning themselves, and smirking at their acquaintances from the vantage of luxurious chariots. It was a scandal, but Madrid grinned, and the patricians of the antediluvian stem confessed themselves beaten.

There was still a lingering fondness for the deposed Isabella among the lower orders. They looked upon her as a good sort, one of the old stock, prayerful, and affable. She was accustomed to enter wayside cabins, and get into homely chat with the peasants. The Italian woman never did that. Alphonse Daudet's description of Isabella as a stout queen, who by her massive jaws and high complexion resembled a coarse-rinded blood-orange, would not be endorsed by these humble yearners after the bygone. Indeed, they regarded her as one who had been a type of beauty in her time, and was still a type of good-nature, and were forgiving to her peccadilloes, she was so devout. Of course I must not be understood as speaking here of Spanish partisans of the Republican idea. They had no more pity for the creatures tainted with Royalty than the Polynesian for his leprous kinsman—but they were comparatively few.

Great Britain, at that period, was represented by Mr. Austin Layard, and the United States by General Daniel Sickles. The British Envoy was in a dilemma; he did not know how far he would be justified in recognising the newly-proclaimed Republic; if he received visits of ceremonial it would be an unpardonable breach of courtesy not to return them; in short, to use a very graphic locution of the masses, he was waiting to see how the cat jumped, and cheerfully submitted to a diplomatic catarrh which confined him to his room. I went to visit him, when we had an interesting dialogue on some recently exhumed relics of antiquity and exquisite bits of crockery-ware. Mr. Layard impressed me as more taken up with concerns of Nineveh and Wardour Street than of *la haute politique*. But, as he frankly acknowledged, he was not free to act until he had received his instructions from Downing Street. Though there is no written pact to the effect, the rule is that Russia, Germany, Austria—the Great Powers in short—shall only act in conjunction, and after having exchanged confidential notes, when eventualities arise affecting all their interests, such as this in Madrid; and—another consideration besides—was there really any Government yet? It was only provisional. It could hardly be supposed that any of the Great Powers would refuse to bow to the will of the Spanish people; but what was its will? That was a question that could not be admitted to be definitely settled.

The United States had struck the key-note—had recognised the infant Republic, while the Prime Minister, Señor Figueras, was waiting for the chorus of acclamation from the "robust voices" of those Great Powers which deliberate before they act. The United States are a fast-trotting buggy; but these Great Powers in this miserable, played-out old Continent are slow coaches. Not that there were not deliberations in the White House before General Sickles was authorized to use his discretionary power in signing the baptismal certificate of this Republic of accident. General Sickles was undoubtedly clever; he had experience in his time as a journalist, an advocate, and a soldier. It was his opinion that Spain had found in the Republic the means of establishing her power and prosperity on a solid basis. During the crisis, he kept his Government informed of what was passing, and to his demand transmitted by cable in the dawn of Wednesday, the 14th of February, an answer was returned within twenty hours, permitting him to exercise his judgment as he thought proper. He imagined that a Federal Republic, on the pattern of that of the United States, with provincial legislatures in Catalonia, Aragon, Andalusia, and so on, and a National Congress in Madrid, was the panacea for the ills of Spain, and that that would be sufficient to dissolve all antagonisms of race, custom, and feeling, and amalgamate them into one accordant patriotic sentiment. The General was over-hopeful in the estimation of others, who knew Spain as well as he; but he acted rightly according to his views, and ably according to his gifts—only it was to be hoped the General would use his influence to dissuade his Government from offending its friends and brothers of Spain by proposing anew a transaction that would lead to the abandonment of Cuba—an awkward mission with which he was once charged. Surely if a diplomatic representative could quietly talk the influential personages of the nation to which he was accredited into a zeal for the abolition of slavery in Porto Rico, he could quietly talk the influential personages of his own nation into letting Spanish territory alone. A pompous man this American Minister, active, talkative, and on cordial terms with himself. He hobbled about on his cork leg, leaning on the arm of his handsome Spanish wife, the second. There was a legend in Madrid that the General had lost his limb in a duel about a lady; there had been a question of petticoats in his career once, but it never entered into the minds of those simple Madrileños that a soldier without a breastful of decorations might have been wounded, as he had been, on the battle-field.

The United States were friendly; but France, Republican France, what was she doing? Why did she delay to move? She, at least, ought to have had some fellow-feeling for another Republic without Republicans. The truth was, M. Thiers could not come to any decision without consulting his Council of Ministers. His action was not quite so unfettered as that of President Grant. This was the more to be regretted that Señor Olózaga recognised the Republic of mob acclamation—that of the 4th September, 1870, in Paris— without hesitation. The same compliment was felt by Spaniards to be due to the Republic of accident.

On the 20th of February, Señor Castelar took a course that might give a galvanic shock to the world of diplomats, but which was worthy of a bold Republican prophet. Since the mountain would not come to Mahomet, Mahomet went to the mountain. In plainer words—but has not one an excuse for being figurative when speaking of Señor Castelar?—the Minister for Foreign Affairs determined to take the bull by the horns (pardon this figure for the sake of its aptness in Spain). The representatives of the Great Powers did not call on him; he called on them. His coy advances were met with frigid politeness. A Madrid paper asserted that "an important and friendly conference" had been held between the Minister and Mr. Layard, which, to say the least, was a *suggestio falsi*. Mr. Layard, as an English gentleman, could not but have received his visitor in a friendly manner; but he kept within the strict line of his very delicate duties with a studious discretion. Señor Castelar saw plainly that events had not prepared the way and made straight the path of the new Republic towards recognition. The Great Powers could not be found fault with, if they were slow to admit to the brotherhood of nations a Republic which had already exhibited within its fortnight's existence what may be literally called two dictatures (those of Señores Rivero and Martos), the abdication of power by a majority, two provisional and two "permanent" Governments, a cabinet of conciliation, and a cabinet of homogeneity, not to mention a round of permutations in the civil governorships of Madrid, and the captain-generalcy of New Castile, and in the commands of the armies of the North and Catalonia.

From the country poured in felicitations to the Republic from hamlet and city, tumid with a rampant joy. These documents emphatically protested that the majority of the population was Republican. Yet talk confidentially to any Spaniard, not actually a Republican propagandist, and not one of the ignorant lower classes of the towns—an average, intelligent, middle-class Spaniard—and he would tell you there were no Republicans in Spain. The thorough frankness with which Spaniards speak of their own country, its divisions and its national faults, is phenomenal. "We are very foolish," they own with a charming candour, but the foreigner had better not chime in with them. They will fire up in an instant. If they are foolish, it is no business of his; Spanish quarrels are conducted precisely on the principles of those between man and wife. The outsider who interposes in them must be prepared to wipe a bloody nose.

But the doctrines of Republicanism were producing their effects in the army nevertheless, and the first of these was a tendency to demoralization. The troops at Barcelona fraternized with the working men, and raised cries for the Republic and for their own liberation from service. They desired individual as well as national independence. In that they were but logical. The Republicans out of power inveighed against standing armies as a monstrosity, a relic of effete Monarchical tyranny. The argument was now used against the Republic; the bird of freedom was menaced by a shaft plumed from her own wing. If discipline were once generally relaxed in the army, which is the salt of Spain, then farewell security and come chaos. That was the chief peril in the way. A man, in the highest meaning of the word, one born to command, was wanted to save the country. He was looked for in vain. Prim had left no successor.

In forming my opinions on Spain and the Spaniards, I was aided not a little by the good offices of a shrewd but eccentric American dentist, named Maceehan, who had left Pennsylvania at so remote a date that nobody could recollect it. Long as he had been absent from his native country, he retained its accent, its peculiarities, and evergreen patriotism, and on each recurring 4th of July gave a lavish banquet in honour of American Independence in a restaurant decked with star-spangled banners, and had the privilege of making all the magnates of the capital, soldiers, ministers, courtiers, nobles, poets, and painters, clink their glasses as he sang "Yankee Doodle." Long as he had been in Madrid, he could not speak Spanish correctly, and his mistakes fed the clubs with side-splitting anecdotes. He was the soul of hospitality, and garrulous as a jay. He was in the secrets of the wire-workers, and had a novel process of extracting information as he extracted teeth. As his patient sat in the chair of torture he plied him slyly with interrogatories, and learned what he wanted, but he never betrayed confidences. In his way he was as proud as the proudest Spaniard of them all. Emilio Castelar came to him once with an agonizing toothache. Maceehan laid hold of the offending fang with his forceps. Castelar shrieked and clutched at his hand.

"You have got the wrong tooth!"

"Caramba!" said the Pennsylvanian, lowering his instrument. "So you have come here to teach me my business. I will thank you to leave the room, señor."

"I beg a thousand pardons, but consider the pain. Do with me as you like, dear doctor."

"The dear doctor in that case will adjourn the operation till to-morrow. By that time the señor may have discovered that though the dear doctor may not be an adept at literature or administration, he has some skill at pulling teeth."

And Castelar, in spite of his apologies and entreaties and plaints, had to accept the penance of four-and-twenty hours. He could not think of going anywhere else, for Maceehan was master of his profession. There was not a set of artificial grinders in Madrid with which the American was not familiar. He had looked into the mouths of every Infante and Infanta, had lanced the gums of awful Captains-General, and inserted gold wires in the ivory treasures of most of the reigning beauties. He had been dentist by appointment to Isabella, and had care of the *mâchoire* of the lovely Eugenia de Montijo in her maidenhood. The very thought of sipping a cup of tea in the intimacy of a man who had fingered the palate of a Cardinal, plugged the hollow in a Queen's molar, and arrested the manifestation of caries in the central incisor of an Empress, was too much. It was oppressive.

I was amply provided with letters of introduction at starting, but I was in no hurry to present them. It was fortunate for me. Those who were in power to-day were in disgrace to-morrow, and *vice versâ*, and most of those to whom I had credentials were leaders of parties. One non-politician, a scion of my own sept, but no relative, I did call upon, as funds were to be forwarded to me through his agency. A pleasant old man, he had a brogue as Irish as the *canavaun* of the Bog of Allen, although he had quitted Ireland in early childhood—a mellow, musical, unctuous brogue. What a sovereign contempt he had for fomenters of revolution, intriguers, and the drones who buzzed while others worked, and wanted to be rewarded for buzzing!

"Namesake," he said, "if you knew the mean secret motives of half these wretched politicians by trade, you would spit upon them. There was but one man fit to govern this nation."

I forget whom he mentioned, but it was a Marshal (Narváez, I fancy), who, when asked on his death-bed by his father-confessor, Did he forgive his enemies? answered that he had none—he had shot them all.

"There may be nothing serious here for the present," he continued, "and yet one can't tell; but I think they will go on shilly-shallying and tinkering up constitutions for months to come."

"Then I should have a better field for my labours in the Carlist country."

"Undoubtedly; but if you think of going there, you must cut off that yellowish-red beard or they will call you Judas Iscariot. Do you speak Basque?"

"No; but as to the beard, I am equal to the sacrifice of shaving it and dying my moustache."

"Ah, yes; you may do that sure enough, but it is not so easy to learn Basque!"

If I could not learn Basque I could learn of the Basques, and what I did learn was so much to their credit that it is only fair to write it down. They were not Thugs, they were neither sanguinary nor thievish. The peasantry of the Basque provinces are the finest in Spain—intelligent, hospitable, brave, gentle, but fiercely fanatical where religion is concerned. Instances were narrated to me of travellers who had been arrested by them, being liberated without damage to person or detriment to purse. In one case a Frenchman was robbed by a small party, but his money and papers were restored to him a few days after by one of the chiefs, with an apology. The correspondent of the *Temps*, who accompanied the army in a previous Carlist campaign, informed me that after a skirmish in which forty Carlists were captured, he was anxious to send an account of the affair to Paris, but he did not know how.

"Hold!" said a colonel, "I'll find you the means."

He called over a prisoner, and asked him if he were let off on parole, would he take a letter through the disturbed district, and post it on the other side for a French gentleman? The man pleaded fatigue.

"You'll be well paid."

At last he consented; my informant gave him the letter and a five-franc piece. While monsieur was searching his pockets for more money to give him, the prisoner said:

"I have no change, caballero; how shall we manage?"

The prisoner duly set off; the letter was duly posted and duly arrived, and the prisoner faithfully returned and delivered himself up. Honour is not yet extinct in the Basque provinces, nor is magnanimity in the Spanish army. The commandant dismissed the peasant with a look of admiration and a push on the back. But some fireside philosopher will argue:

"Why, these honourable fellows cut telegraph wires and fire on railway trains."

The Carlists explain: "The telegraph and the railway are our greatest enemies; the one sends for reinforcements, the other brings them."

The unfortunate station-masters are to be pitied. Lizárraga sends one word that he will incur the penalty of death if he makes up a train for troops. The troops arrive, their commander demands to be furnished with a train to take him to a certain point; if the station-master refuses he is not merely threatened with the death-penalty, but incurs it on the spot. But the fireside philosophers, assuming the cocked-hat of the general, will continue:

"Why not protect the telegraphs and the railways?" The query may be met, *more Hibernico*, by another:

Do the philosophers know how enormous and difficult an extent of country has to be protected?

It would take more men than there are in the Spanish army altogether, including the regiment of dismissed generals in Madrid, to act as military milesmen in the perturbed territory. The Army of the North did what it could—that is to say, it fortified the railway stations, converting them into veritable block-houses, and supplied escorts to the trains; but the Carlists had an unpurchasable ally in the darkness. They could come down in the night and play old Harry with metals and wires. The insurgents were ill-armed and undisciplined, but they were on their own ground, every square inch of which they knew; they were leal to each other, and they had acquired the secret of guerrilla campaigning—that is, they harassed the regulars by fighting and running away, so that they might live to fight another day. They avoided concentration in mass, knowing how dangerous it is to pack all one's eggs in a single basket.

So daring had these Carlists become that bands had made demonstrations in perilous nearness to the capital, or rather they had been organized in the capital itself and had taken to the field in the neighbourhood. From a rising ground hard by the palace could be distinguished with the naked eye a thicket on the desolate plain in the distance, where the remnants of one band were known to be hiding. The fates were against the insurgents, as they were met at Buendia and badly beaten two days after they had unfurled the banner of revolt. Eleven of them were slain, including a priest, twenty wounded and one hundred and seventeen taken prisoners, including their two chiefs. The elder of these, Alonso, a man of three-score and ten, died in the military hospital of Madrid on the 19th of March. He was a venerable fanatic of asinine stupidity to have risked a fight with regular troops in the open. Fortune, in my experience, favours not so much the brave as the wary. Had this particular Alonso the brave, really an Alonso the reckless, availed himself of a few picks and spades—the first farmhouse will seldom fail to supply entrenching tools—he might have lived to die in his own bed of a natural disease.

CHAPTER V.

A Late Capital—The Gambling Mania—A French Rendezvous—The Duke de Fitzpepper—The Morality of Passing Bad Money—Spanish Compliments—Men in Pickle—A Licentious Ballet—Federal Manners—Prim's Artifice—Nouvilas Goes North—A Carlist Proclamation—Don Alfonso—Midnight Oil—Castelar's Circular.

MADRID is not an early capital—natural effect of the climate. In the middle of the day the blinds are let down, the shops are shut, the streets are empty—everybody who can at all manage it is taking the siesta. The business of sunlight is at a standstill. The few hours thus stolen from the day are religiously made restitution of to the night, which is undoubtedly the most agreeable period for a stroll. Pleasure is in full swing, the promenades are alive, flirtation is methodically practised in the Spanish way—that is, through an intervening lattice—theatres and ball-rooms contribute to the programme of diversion, the coffee-houses (where chocolate is mostly consumed) are packed to the door-posts, and the business of gaslight is prosecuted with a desperate concentration of energy and a brooding perseverance.

The business of gaslight, unfortunately, is high play. That is one of the social curses of Spain. Everybody gambles, to the sentries in the guard-house, the patients in the hospitals, the felons in the gaols. Such is the overwhelming dominion of this national passion that I should not be surprised at reading of a condemned man on his way to the garrote craving a hand of cards with the executioner to distract him from his sorrows. Strained the situation was at this crisis, and in all the clubs the cards were thrown on the tables with a fever as of men seeking some relaxation from the fierce game of politics; but, as I had opportunity to assure myself afterwards, this was nothing exceptional. The fever for play as high as the pocket can allow, often higher, is normal. The foreigner—and all foreigners provided with the slightest credentials are most graciously made free of the clubs—soon takes note of that.

The Fornos, the Suizo, and other coffee-houses were transformed into debating-forums, and sometimes I frequented them to catch what was going on; but my haunt of predilection was a restaurant patronized by French refugees. They had brought with them the Gaulish gaiety, and it was instructive to see Communists, fugitive aristocrats, bagmen with the asphalte of the boulevards still clinging to the soles of their boots, and steady old settlers in Madrid foregathering in friendly forgetfulness of differing shades of political coats. One of the three Marquesses de Fonvielle and de Coutuly, of the *Temps*, amongst other journalists, used to drop in regularly. De Coutuly has since strayed into diplomacy. Touching journalists who wander into that luxurious labyrinth, the representative of the *New York Herald*, at Madrid, a painstaking gentleman with a certain cleverness, Russell Young, subsequently became United States' Minister to China. Prizes of this class, which rain upon Continental and American publicists, seldom fall to the lot of their brethren of the British press, unless they get into Parliament or boldly single themselves out from the anonymous herd. Then they are sometimes promoted to a Consulship in an insalubrious region, where they have every facility for studying the manners of the buck-nigger, and the customs of the lively sand-fly. Far and away the most interesting customer of this restaurant was the Duke de Fitzpepper, a tall, dark, strong man with curly black hair, a boisterous voice, and a bold laugh. He had to quit France on account of an affair of honour. He had been in the Imperial Navy, had a squabble with his captain, and resigned his commission that he might send him a challenge. They met with the customary duelling swords, but de Fitzpepper made a mistake. He ran his antagonist through. I know naught of the merits of the quarrel, but to my insularly uneducated mind it appeared that the gallant nobleman experienced inadequate remorse at having the blood of a fellow-creature on his soul. Perhaps I am hyper-sensitive, but when de Fitzpepper used to boast "*Je me connais dans le flingot*," it sent a thread of cold water creeping down my spine, not from fear but from aversion. Yet it was impossible to keep aloof from him for long, he was such a joyous, dashing, carry-your-outworks pattern of a musketeer.

Evil associations corrupt good manners, I suppose, which must be the excuse for a Frenchman with whom I entered into conversation in this mirthful caravanserai. I happened to show him a coin which had been passed upon me, an escudo, which would be worth a sovereign if it were not counterfeit.

"What a shame!" he exclaimed as he fingered it. "What are you going to do with it?"

"Nothing," I said. "It's useless to me."

"Lend it to me, pray."

I gave it to him, and the following night he asked me what commission I would allow him. He had passed the bad escudo in his turn. I was indignant, and accused him of having been guilty of a dishonest act. I would touch none of the proceeds of his crookedness.

"Nonsense!" he said, astonished. "I got rid of it in a hell. They're all rogues there when they have a chance."

I submit to the casuists that this was a very nice case of conscience. Winning money at cards is not earning it. He who seeks to win it is demoralized, and it is to his advantage and the advantage of society that he should be discouraged in his pernicious foolishness. Therefore, q.e.d., it was commendable to palm that base coin upon him. I was unequal to deciding the question off-hand, so I elected to take not a real of the Frenchman's equivocal profit. But if the Frenchman was to blame, was I not responsible in the first instance, as having afforded him the means of cheating his neighbour? When the casuists shall have elucidated this riddle to their satisfaction, perhaps they will oblige by telling me how many thousand angels could alight on the point of a needle.

Morality is at a low ebb in Madrid, or rather the moral code is regulated by notions peculiar to the latitude. So with habits. A man must be "native and to the manner born," before he can affect competency to interpret them. For example, when a Madrileño asseverates that his house is yours, or that his equipage which you so much admire is at your disposal, he does not intend that you should take up your residence with him there and then, or hold his coachman at your beck. It is simply a form of etiquette, a mode of speech, as of the Englishman of past generations who challenged you to mortal combat and subscribed himself "your obedient humble servant." You will be guilty of a grave solecism if you imitate that American to whom the grandee remarked with effusion that the stud which captivated his taste was his own, his very own.

"Thanks," said Brother Jonathan; "I'll take the roan and the chestnut to-day and call for the others to-morrow!"

Although a man may tender you fraudulent coinage with a brazen front, he may be keen in honour, and resent an insult to his sister with a knife-stab; although he may intrigue for a Government place with a slimy self-abasement, under circumstances the same being may go forth unflinchingly and sacrifice himself on the altar of his country. Spain is the home of paradox. The beggar is addressed as "your worship," mutiny is a venial offence, bribery of officials is a recognised prescription. At the very epoch of which I write, the murderers of Prim were stalking about the capital; it was a town-crier's secret who they were and who was the personage who was their employer, yet none had the temerity to denounce them. And in the saladero, or the "salting-tub," as the prison was called, it was notorious that there were malefactors who gave lessons in forgery, and who positively utilized their cells as convenient head-quarters from which to prey on the unwary public. Their plan was to write to somebody of position, whose name they had lighted on in a directory, and inform him that they had often heard speak of him as a citizen of integrity, and felt that they might trust him; they were singularly situated, immured for a debt of a few duros, and yet in the vicinity of his residence they were cognizant of an immense buried treasure; if he would only send them the trifle needful to pay off that debt and cover their fare to his town, they would take him with them to the site of the secret hoard, and repay him with interest for his kindness. This transparent ruse actually told with hundreds of dupes. How the *auri sacra fames* will deprive sane men of sense! He would be a spendthrift of sympathy who would waste his sympathy upon them.

I had been under the impression that Spain was a deeply religious country. The impression was illusive. It may be fanatically religious in parts, but too often the educated classes rail at religion. As comes to pass when inordinate demand has been made on credulity, a reaction arises, and those whose faith was implicit yesterday become the scoffing heretics of to-day. The tide has turned, and it is no unfrequent occurrence to hear a Spaniard declare he is not a Christian, whose fathers would have perhaps burned at a stake the wretch who would have dared to utter such a profanity. This is very bad. One extreme is as wicked as another. If the Scylla of stupid superstition was dangerous, the Charybdis of arrogant scepticism is destructive. This is essentially a Roman Catholic country, yet never have I seen anywhere, in the lands where Roman Catholicism is disliked and contemned even, the ceremonies and institutions of the Church treated with more undisguised ribaldry. I went to the Novedades, a popular theatre in a humble quarter of the town in the vicinity of the Calle de Toledo, to see what the piece on the occasion, "El Triunfo de la República," was like. I got in as a "Carlist ballet" was being danced; two men were dressed to represent two famous cabecillas, Saballs and a colleague, two others to represent the Carlist priest, Santa Cruz, and a monk of the party. Santa Cruz was bulky as Friar Tuck, leered from under his scoop hat, drank wine, reeled, toddled, fell, and kicked up his heels as the wild Mabille quadrille music was played; and high was the content and noisily expressed the delight of the audience. The four women who took part in the Terpsichorean orgie wore the robes of nuns, and must have belonged to the order of Sisters of Shame, if to any. They had blue hoods, white bands across their foreheads and bosoms, red crosses wrought on their habits, and trailing skirts of white. Their dancing was not voluptuous; it would be a misnomer to let it down with so mild an epithet; it was grossly indecent. They exposed their limbs, and the audience was ecstatic at the sight. Not a murmur of censure was to be heard. And this bacchanalian riot, too obscene for any self-respecting house of ill-fame, was supposed to be held in a church. The scenery showed a mockery of ecclesiastical architecture and pious pictures. As a dramatic effort, "El Triunfo de la República" was very poor. Zorilla was caricatured as a fox (a play upon his name), and Sagasta as a devil-fish, and the apotheosis revealed the Genius of Spain waving a flag lettered with the words, "Viva la República Federal!" The flag was welcomed with vehement cheers, in affirmation that those who looked on and admired the burlesque of ministers of the national faith were all stout Federal Republicans, corresponding somewhat to the Communists of the Paris of two years before.

These Federals, I own, I do not like. A deputation of them from the provinces arrived one of these evenings, and put up at the Fonda de Paris. They were scrubby louts, smoked between the courses although ladies were at table, which, however, could be condoned, as it was Spanish. But they also wore their hats. That irritated one guest, and he called to a waiter to bring him a hat which he would find on a peg outside. Having been handed his head-gear, he clapped it on, and said that was all he wanted. The hint was not lost. The boors dined in a room by themselves during the rest of their stay. And yet these Federal Republicans profess to respect public opinion; but by the phrase must be understood the opinion of those who agree with them. The Intransigentes, on whose support they depend, have arms in their hands, and will try to keep them. Only one man was ever able to disarm them, and he was assassinated. If Prim did not know the Spanish mind intuitively, and as no other man ever knew it, even he would not have succeeded. After the promiscuous distribution of arms to the multitude had been made from the windows of the storehouses in Madrid at the close of 1868, he tried every means to get them back, but to no purpose. Promises of rewards to those who would give up the guns were useless; threats and coaxings were in vain. At last Prim hit on a notable scheme. At a review he publicly insulted the corps he was so long trying to disembody; he either rode past them without noticing them, or made remarks on their appearance the reverse of complimentary. The officers threw up their commissions in dudgeon; they had served the cause of the people faithfully, and were not to be treated with contempt; they would no longer carry arms for such ungrateful friends. It was just what Prim wanted.

While Madrid was thus seething and bubbling as if it were on the verge of boiling over, and the great question of elections for the new Cortes to determine the future "permanent" style of administration was being mooted, the Carlists were plucking up heart and maturing their designs. They fancied they would soon have the nation before them the *nudum et cœcum corpus* of Sylla's description—defenceless and blind. Nouvilas, one of the numberless generals of Spain, was ordered to the north. At a Republican meeting before his departure, he promised that he would take his five sons with him to fight against the Carlists. At the same meeting he declared himself the uncompromising enemy of all dictatorships, and warned those who expected that he would use his power in that sense not to make a mistake. He was a soldier, not a politician, and the day that the Republic would be consolidated, and peace secured, he would retire into private life. It did not seem as if peace were shortly to be secured. There was a proposition to raise fifty battalions of free corps to crush the insurgents. The only difficulty in the way was the loan for their armaments. The battalions were to be organized by provinces, and each was to be composed of 900 men (making a total of 44,100), and to be officered from the reserve. The proposition of itself was sufficient to wake the fools out of their paradise. These Carlists were not to be underrated. If they could do nothing else, they could issue proclamations. They were great at these. They promised to give the army the "licencia absoluta" which some soldiers demanded from the Republic at Barcelona. One Ramon V. Valcarces, commandant-general of the province of Lugo, was exceedingly anxious that the Galicians should come out to conquer or die. He told them that the national banner of their legitimate King waved triumphantly in the provinces of Catalonia, Castile, Leon, the Asturias, and the Vasco-Navarre, which was a piece of bounce—legitimate, may it be called?—on his part; and added scathingly that the Government at Madrid was in the hands of a group of adventurers, who called themselves Spaniards and Liberals. Those impostors would raise the taxes until it would be impossible to pay them, would sell the Antilles and persecute religion.

Tidings were wafted to us mysteriously that the brother of the legitimate King, H.R.H. Don Alfonso, of Bourbon and Lorraine, had held a review of the forces of Saballs at Vidra, in Catalonia. His Royal Highness was accompanied by his wife, the Doña Maria. His Royal Highness wore flesh-coloured riding breeches with black stripes, jack-boots, a zamarra or sheep-skin upper garment, and a flat white cap of the make of those used by Scotch shepherds. Doña Maria wore a cap of the same kind, with a gold tassel coquettishly falling over her left shoulder. The august pair were mounted, and the lady, who chivalrously accompanied her husband, witched the Carlists with noble horsemanship. Don Alfonso was surrounded by a brilliant staff, conspicuous amongst whom was a son of that Don Enrique of Bourbon who was shot in a duel by the Duke of Montpensier.

The "only court" did not lack a moidering liveliness. Of nights I usually leant by my balcony overlooking the Puerta del Sol, and watched the frail sodality of the Moon prowling about in charge of the superfluous duenna, the while the brawl of palaver, the cries of "água fresca," or of the last edition of the *Correspondencia*, the "theeah" in such wise cadenced, or the boom of the watchman's voice came floating upwards, before I sat me down to a hard spell of work, sifting grain from chaff, and committing my thoughts to paper, a moistened towel round my temples, and a pot of black coffee at my elbow. The sun was usually ogling the fountain in the Plaza before I had finished.

The burden of work imposed upon the correspondent who desired to be loyal to duty was weighty on occasion. For example, late on the 26th of February the official journal came out with a lengthy circular from Don Emilio Castelar, to the representatives of Spain abroad. The object was to obtain the recognition of the Republic by Powers other than the United States and Switzerland. I saw the importance of sending a translation of this pregnant State paper at once, and shut myself up in my room with a supply of pens, ink, and paper, and the indispensable coffee-pot. I was not an accomplished Spanish scholar, but with the aid of a youthful groundwork in Latin, a fair knowledge of Italian, a familiarity with French, and a dictionary, I succeeded in turning out a full, accurate—nay, I will say a vivid—rendering of this historic composition before I unlocked my door, and transmitted it to London within twelve hours. Spanish is not difficult. If Italian is the daughter of Latin, Spanish is the son. And with energy and mother-wit, one can do much.

Castelar's was a brilliant and sustained effort; but it read more like an essay by Macaulay than a diplomatic holograph. It was splendid, but it was not official. It lacked crispness, and dealt in excessive rhetoric from the phrase in an opening paragraph where it spoke of Spain assuming a place in the Amphictyonic council of Europe, to the closing sentence. The fall of the Monarchy was traced to the hour when the institution solemnly ceded its own country to the foreigner (alluding to the pitiful abdication of Charles IV. in favour of his "friend and ally" Napoleon, at Bayonne in 1808). True, attempts had been thrice made since to revive the old system with a new spirit, but they had failed; in 1812, the Democratic Monarchy; in 1837, the Parliamentary Monarchy; in 1869, the Elective Monarchy. The former order of things disappeared through inherent domestic causes; the Republic appeared of its own virtue, by the law of necessity. In 1869 the Constituent Cortes had proclaimed a Monarchy for three fundamental reasons: firstly, because it corresponded with the traditions of the Spanish people; secondly, because they believed it would secure liberal principles; and thirdly, because it would harmonize their form of government with that existing in nearly every part of Europe. The trouble was where to find the monarch. They had no dynasty typifying religious and national principles united to modern spirit like that of England, no princes like those who had built up the unity of Italy and of Germany on battlefields; their sovereign houses presented no stability. They had to look outside for a king, at the double risk of disturbing the peace of Europe and wounding the national sentiment. They found him in the scion of an illustrious line, united to France by the war of 1859, to Prussia by the war of 1866, to Great Britain by the establishment of parliamentary rule in Italy. But the national sentiment of Spain was against him. It left him in a solitude that was asphyxia. At last he renounced a crown of which he only felt the weight on his brow and not the dignity in his soul. When he left, this Government came not by violent revolution, but by logical evolution. The Republic was not provisional, but definitive. (As if there were any finality in politics!) The Cortes which had proclaimed it were the most permanent estate in the nation, inasmuch as when others melted away they remained. It was the same Cortes which undertook the national defence in the epic years from 1808 to 1814, which abrogated the rights of Don Carlos to the ancient crown, and which sanctioned the dethronement of the Bourbons. Spain owed the change she had effected to no cosmopolitan influences or agitations. She sought autonomy, not Utopianism; she coveted no conquest, but she wished to show that she was living, not dead; that she was still great, but not with the greatness of ruin, like the empires buried under the valleys of Asia.

There was an excellent thickset gentleman in Madrid, a literary pluralist, who combined the offices of "own correspondent" to several London journals. He was a diligent "snapper-up of unconsidered trifles," who would never set even the Manzanares on fire. He met me after I had despatched my version of Castelar's circular, and was cooling my aching brain on the shady side of the Puerta del Sol.

"Did you read that thing of 'Musica's'?" he said. ("Musica" was the nickname of the silver-tongued professor-politician.)

"Yes; lovely and long and flimsy as a rainbow," I remarked.

"I think you ought to send an epitome of it to London."

"I shall not."

"Well, I may tell you Chose is sending the whole of it on," he continued.

Chose was a most formidable rival.

"Who translated it for him?" I asked.

"As it is very important I am getting my sons to do it. Indeed, he asked me."

"And you never told me."

"Ah! you see, he has a reputation to sustain."

"And I have a reputation to make."

"I'll let you have a *précis* to-morrow."

"No, thanks," I answered, turning on my heel.

The thickset gentleman looked mighty blank when he gazed on the paper a few days after with my translation covering nearly two columns of small type, nor did his astonishment lessen when I confided to him that it had been made for me by the Man in the Moon.

CHAPTER VI.

Warning to Ladies—The Hotel Parliament—An Anglo-Spanish Mentor—The Evil Genii of the Monarchy—The Curses of Spain—Government and Religion Affairs of Climate—The Carlists, Norwegians, and English, all Republicans!—Notions on Heredity—The Five Spanish Parties—The Army the Lever of Power—The Student-Cæsar—Order *versus* Republic—The Chained Colours—Dorregaray's Appeal to the Soldiers—Influence of the Church—Wanted: a Benevolent Despot.

IN the first line, it may be generous to warn ladies (if any of the gentler sex there be among my readers) to skip this chapter. There will be no indelicate disclosures—not that indelicate disclosures would bar the inquisitiveness of some females, judging by the ingenuity with which they intrigue for seats at the trials in the Divorce Court, and the avidity with which they devour "spicy," that is scandalous, details; but matter of a political, speculative, and quasi-philosophical nature is to be discussed, and I fear me much it will be dry and prosy.

A shady little room in one of the upper stories of the Fonda de Paris was used as reading-room. It was thickly carpeted, the walls were covered with oil paintings in massive ornamented frames, and on the tables were placed curious jars, antique candlesticks, bronze statuettes, damascened daggers, and what is known as the merchandise of *bijouterie* and *vertu*. There were few papers there, and but one book, a Spanish Army List in gorgeous green velvet cover with gilt clasps. In fact, it was more of an auctioneer's private show-room than *cabinet de lecture*, for the Brothers Fallola were dealers in *bric-à-brac*, and could not forego the chance of poking their wares under the notice of their customers. The Italian is first cousin to the Hebrew.

We held a grave Parliament of our own in this little room, and there I made the acquaintance of an English settler in Spain—an elderly gentleman who had been engaged in mining. He was well educated, had travelled widely, was pronounced in his views, and as he expressed them with candour and was possessed of a high order of intelligence, I listened to him with attention. Indeed, we all accepted him as Mentor. He indoctrinated me into the knotty catechism of Spanish politics.

Broadly speaking, he maintained that the monarchy was its own greatest enemy. It had fallen because of its indifference to public opinion. Among its evil genii were the pastrycook Marforio, Father Claret, and Sister Patrocinio. The birth of a daughter to Ferdinand VII., fault of nature, was the primal fatality. As Count O'Neil remarked when he heard the natal salute stop at the nineteenth cannon-shot, unhappy Spain was doomed, because of the gender of the newly-born, to be over-shadowed with the pall of grief and mourning. But the primal error was the unnatural marriage of Isabella to her cousin, Don Francisco. Never was there a more ill-assorted union. A woman of ardent temperament and strong fibre was allied to a feeble nonentity without sap or spirit. Had she become the spouse of a man like Victor Emmanuel, things might have gone better.

Spain was a grand country, he held, one of the richest in creation in minerals, forests, vineyards, orchards, silk and flocks. The people were a people that improved upon intercourse, and had some grand qualities. But the curses of Spain were the ignorance of the masses, the greed of the professional politicians, and the varying ascendancy of some one man's power in the army.

"Was the country ripe for its existing form of government?" I asked.

"Government," said he, "like religion, is very much a matter of birth and training, or, to put it more briefly, of climate. The circumcision of Judaism, the ablutions of Mahometanism, are the simple useful dictates of some wise man skilled in sanitary science. People of warm southern natures crave light and colour and music in worship; in colder lands, with dispositions hardier and less imaginative, they are satisfied with severe forms——"

"I know all those theories about religion," I interrupted, "but I am anxious to have your judgment on government."

"Identically the same—affair of climate. Those who have to brave privations and work hard for a living are Republicans; the Swiss, for example, the Norwegians, and the Carlists."

"The Carlists! I thought they were Royalists."

The Mentor laughed as he said, "Royalists! why, they are the only Republicans in this land. Have you not heard of their fueros? They reject the tax of blood—they will have no unwilling soldiers taken from their midst. So Republican are they that they will not tolerate a Bishop in their ecclesiastical organization, strict Catholics though they profess themselves. He of Seo de Urgel is the nearest Bishop to their territory, and his diocese is properly in Andorra."

"But the Norwegians are Monarchists," I ventured.

"In name only, as the English are. There is no more democratic administration in the world than that of king-ruled Norway; and in England you are likewise a Republic—that is, you enjoy Republican freedom, only you choose to call the President a Queen. The Queen is but a figure-head, the vivified Union Jack. The Prime Minister, that is to say the elect of the people, not the Queen, sways the genuine wand of power."

"And the House of Lords, the most Conservative hereditary legislature in Europe, how do you account for its existence in this British Republic?" I hazarded as a clincher.

"An accident, my dear sir," he replied, as he pulled at his cigarette. "Like that puff of smoke, it has no power; it is but vapour, and like vapour it will disappear some day, to be succeeded by a Senate on the French or American model. Life-peerages can be justified; the hereditary principle has been tried and found wanting. The male offspring of a jockey are not necessarily skilful horsemen; the son of a fencing-master may be an awkward butter-fingers; the daughter of a *prima ballerina* may be a cripple."

I passed that figure of speech about the vapour, though disciplined vapour drives a locomotive. But I urged, "Do you not believe in blood? Would you place the descendant of a line of brave and cultured men, with traditions to look back upon, on the same level with Bill Sykes or a Bosjesman? Is a game-cock a dunghill? Is a thoroughbred a plough-horse?"

"R-o-t, rot, my dear sir," said Mentor, with an irritating coolness. "Of game-cocks I know nothing; but as far as your horse argument goes, I am prepared to meet you. Care is taken that the mare shall be mated with the proper sire, so that the qualities long worked up to, by judicious crossing, shall not be lost or deteriorated; but there is no such selection in the case of a lord; he follows his own figary, and his figary is usually money, to regild a faded shield. Blood, sir, has less to do with those things than education and the associations of childhood. Send an earl's son to St. Giles', and he will grow up a saucy gutter-boy; send a burglar's son to Eton, and he may develop into what is conventionally recognised as a gentleman."

There was no arguing down our Mentor on this point, so the subject was changed, and he tried to disintegrate the ingredients in the very mixed dish of Spanish parties—a complete olla podrida. There were five factions in the distracted State, two schools of Monarchists and three of Republicans. These were—1st, the Alfonsists, or those who wished that the son of the deposed Queen should be raised to the throne; 2nd, the Legitimists or Carlists (embracing a large body of the clergy); 3rd, the Republicans of long standing, who were actually in power; 4th, the ex-Monarchists—the neo-Republicans or Radicals, who sometimes called themselves Progresistas, and favoured the United Republic; and 5th, the Intransigentes, or the Irreconcilables, the extreme of the extreme, who clamoured for a Federal Republic.

"As example of that ignorance of the masses of which I spoke," said Mentor, "the mob of Madrid is fiercely Federal, which proves that it does not know what Federalism is; for one of the first results of Federalism would be to reduce this capital to the plane of a third-rate provincial town. Federalism is Spanish dismemberment. If such a system were adopted, you would have a

Royalist North, a Red Republican Catalonia, and a pauperized Castile, politically piebald. Catalonia is Federal, in which Catalonia writes itself down ass, for that province is manufacturing, and with the downfall of protection its prosperity must depart."

"Is there any chance of Amadeus being coaxed back?"

He laughed a laugh that embarrassed me.

"A kick is not soon forgotten, for it is always an insult even when administered with an embroidered slipper."

"What do you think of the situation at the moment?" (This was in the first week of March.)

"Madrid," he answered, "is a hot-bed of political intrigue, and a complicated intrigue is in act of being developed at present. This, I take it, is a fair estimate of the situation. The men in office are controlled by fears of the violent Republicans outside, whom they are powerless to keep under; and the Radicals are anxious to get into office to restrain these same violent Republicans, but hesitate because of the apprehension that they have not sufficient material force behind them. They would fain climb, but that they fear to fall. Thus, as you perceive, the disorganization of the army is at the bottom of all the difficulties, for that it is which leaves the mastery with the dreaded Intransigents. Those, the 'partisans of action' as they are aptly called sometimes, have more energy than either the Ministry or the Radicals, and if this dilly-dallying goes on much longer they may make a bold attempt to get the reins into their own hands. The Radicals are opposed to a dissolution of the Assembly because they fear the Reds would command the polls at the new elections, and go in for sweeping changes on the model of their predecessors in Paris. The present Ministers have not the vigour to check the manœuvring that would bring about such an occurrence, and the Radicals believe that they only could oppose and beat down the fanatics of Communistic proclivities. There are cynics, however, who sneer at patriotic affirmations, and whisper that loaves and fishes have more to do with them than love of country."

I reflected that patriotism of that order was not an exclusively Iberian production, but that possibly the cynics were disappointed politicians themselves.

"The state of the army," resumed Mentor, "is the question after all. A great portion of the rank and file are violently Republican, and one cause of insubordination is that the privates do not believe in the Republicanism of their officers. Of course, the object of the Ministry in raising the proposed battalions of volunteers, is less to put down Carlism than to have a force to fall back upon in case of the army giving itself furlough. I have reason to know that one Minister at least is very uneasy on account of the want of discipline of the troops, and urges upon his colleagues that their first labour should be devoted to repressing all signs of disorder. But the fight for place at Madrid has more interest for them, and the army is melting away. When Ministers make up their minds to a rigorous supervision of the soldiery, there may be no soldiers to supervise."

It dawned upon me that Spaniards, although enjoying the reputation of being quick with lethal weapons under the spur of sudden passion, were very slow in taking ordinary resolutions. "Mañana" is the watchword of the nation: a favourite proverb is twisted into "Never do to-day what you can possibly put off till to-morrow." As a French writer wittily observed, the chariot of State in Spain is fashioned of tortoise-shell and drawn by snails.

"What do you think of Castelar?"

"Castelar!" echoed the Mentor, with a shoulder-movement of compassionate irony, "honest, but weak. He is too good, too single-minded, too amiable, too much of a student to play the Cæsar. Picture to yourself a doctrinaire who can quote Aristotle in the Chamber, while his country is travelling the road to ruin. Poor Señor Castelar is not the coming man."

"And where may we look for him?" I asked.

"Quien sabe? At this moment he may be waxing his moustache in the Balearic Islands, or sipping chocolate in the coffee-house on the ground-floor."

That coffee-house was always full at the juncture. Indeed, to one who had not been made stoical by familiarity with excitements, the tokens of the atmosphere were portentous. Congress often sat under the protection of an armed guard. The crowds in the streets were always large. The talk was of bloodshed; but I had grown so sceptical that I would hardly believe in bloodshed in Madrid until what looked a liquid red had been chemically analyzed and proved to be blood. We had false alarms every other night, and shops were shut for an hour or two; but we got no nearer to revolution than the discussions of sundry excited parliaments over the marble-topped tables. There Spaniards flushed purple, and gesticulated violently over their temperate glasses of sweetened water. What a blessing this is not a whisky-drinking country!

"No," continued the Mentor; "Castelar is the least of all fitted to govern Spain. This people requires to be ruled by stern will and strong grip. The result of handing it over to a weak administration is palpable. Of all nations of the world, Spain is least prepared for Republicanism, and the theoretical Republicans who essayed to control her, in an evil moment for themselves, must before this have discovered the gross blunder they have made. The Republic is a splendid word; but Order is a word more wholesome. The present so-called rulers are incapable of preserving order. They sowed the wind when they taught the soldiers to be malcontent under the Monarchy, because an army was an artificial need in a free nation. Now that the soldiers are taking them at their word, they are reaping the whirlwind. They promised Spain liberty, and Spain, from every indication, is about to enjoy a spell of license. Heaven knows how it will all end; but those who have acutely watched changes like this in other countries are not slow to tell us that we shall have anarchy first to the full."

"And then?" I inquired, "for anarchy is no remedy. It is never final. What shall we have after that?"

"Perhaps a Conservative Republic, but more likely an iron despotism, the dominance of some successful General who has the knack of answering his opponents by ordering their heads to be sliced off."

"Is not that General as likely as not to come from the Carlist camp?" I demanded.

Mentor shook his head in a decisive negative. "No," he said; "outside the northern and a portion of the eastern provinces, Carlism has no solidity."

"But may not the name of Dorregaray, who has crossed the frontier again, turn out to be a spell-word? They tell me he distinguished himself in the war with Morocco."

"Yes," assented Mentor, "he commanded a regiment of galley-slaves there."

"And," I continued, "in Cuba at the outbreak of hostilities he was to the fore."

"True, true; but I would not give that," and he snapped his fingers, "for the fidelity of such as Dorregaray. He served under Don Carlos in the civil war from 1836 to 1840, and that did not hinder him from donning a uniform under Isabella. Cosas de España! Have you never heard of Piquero? His action is a pretty fair criterion of the political morality of your ordinary ambitious Spanish soldier."

No, the man's name was new to me.

"Well, he commanded the regiment of Malaga when Ferdinand VII. returned from France and was made absolute monarch. General Piquero, as soon as he got wind of the decree of absolutism, thought he would be first to curry favour at Court, and sent an address to the palace, praying that his regiment might have the honour of wearing chains emblazoned on the colours in testimony of attachment to the King. The prayer was magnanimously acceded to, and the chains were absolutely borne on the colours for years. Yet not very long afterward this Piquero, this mean, fawning cur, changed front and became a yelping hungry mastiff of democracy. I don't anticipate Dorregaray would play that part."

"Anyhow," I persisted, "the Carlist General has sent forth a manifesto in his self-assumed capacity of commander-in-chief of the Vascongadas and Navarre to the soldiers of the Spanish army. He calls upon them to lay down their arms, promising them free discharges if they desire it, but promotion, decorations, and rewards if they join his standard. What do you think of that?"

"I do not blame him," said Mentor. "In thus tempting the army, he is only doing as every military chief who has ever lifted himself to power by a pronunciamiento has done. The sergeants and corporals are invariably lured with the bait that they shall be made captains and lieutenants, the common soldiers that their pay and rations shall be increased. Such men as go over to Dorregaray only act as too many of their predecessors have acted. In this instance they have an excuse; they can say, 'We were Royalist soldiers a few weeks ago; we are transformed into Republican soldiers now. Our will was never consulted. We are Royalist still, therefore we rally to Don Carlos, who represents the principle of Monarchy.' They could say this, but I am far from thinking they will. Spaniards of the rank and file do not chop logic; it is the non-commissioned officers who initiate mutinies for purposes of personal advancement; the private is a machine, not a thinking bayonet."

In response to my inquiry as to the influence which remained to the Church, my Mentor shook his head, and said outside the hilly regions where Carlism prevailed, and the remote rural districts, it was next to null, save among the more comfortable class of women. The common Spaniard took his faith as he would his heritage; he was a Christian because his fathers were so before him—it was an affair of family—and his calling himself a Christian, which signifies Christian exclusively of the Roman Catholic persuasion, is a survival of the thoughts bequeathed by the Saracenic occupation. He who was not a Christian was a "Moro," and to this day the Jew or the Protestant is a Moor, tarred with the same brush as the turbaned Islamite.

"The Church," concluded Mentor, "is not to blame if it bums incense and assaults Heaven with prayers for such a change of Government as will bring money to its coffers. If the Republic last, the Church will be separated from the State, and every congregation will have to pay its own minister. That would be frank, at all events; but so long as there is a State religion, the ministers of which are supposed to be paid, it is a scandal not to pay them, and their reverences are perfectly right to turn Carlist or Alfonsist."

After these discussions in the reading-room I sometimes felt as if I had been endeavouring to unravel the Schleswig-Holstein tangle. Was I not right in warning off the ladies? Truly, Spanish politics are confusing. My usual reflections upon them resolved themselves into the uneasy conviction that they were a Lincoln morass overlaid by a London fog, and that it would be a joy to have some thousands of Will-o'-the-Wisp guides prisoned to the chins in the quagmire, and replaced by one benevolent despot bearing the light with strong, sure grasp.

CHAPTER VII.

The Carnival—About Kissing Feet—Mummers and Masquers—The Paseo de Recoletos—The Writer is taken for Cluseret—Incongruity in Costume—Shrove Tuesday—Panic on the Prado—A Fancy Ball—The "Entierro de la Sardina"—Lenten Amusements—A Spanish Mystery—"Pasion y Muerte de Jesus"—Of the Stage Stagey—Critical Remarks.

SIMULTANEOUSLY with the Ministerial crisis we were tortured by the throes of the Carnival, which was a trial too great for a Republic so young. But the weather came to the aid of the powers that were, and prevented the festival from rising to a height of merriment when it might become tumultuous. The opening day was one of leaden skies and moist pavements in the forenoon, of little patches of ultramarine above and little eruptions of noise below in the afternoon. There is one consolation on a wet day—you can conveniently make inspection of the extremities of dear womankind. I no longer elevate my eyebrows at the Spanish formula of compliment to the mistress of one's affections—"I kiss your feet." Anyone could kiss them with pleasure; they are so tiny, shapely, and sylph-like. There surely are the "little mice" of Suckling's ballad! Atalanta must have had ankles like those revealed under the lifted skirts of the doncella yonder, Cinderella such another pair of arched insteps. But one cannot contemplate them for ever, bitten by the statuary's mania for the symmetric though he be.

On the second morning, there was a light grey fog, like the smoke after gunpowder, on the square called "The Gate of the Sun." I have tasted the joys of Carnival elsewhere—at Rome in Papal times and at Paris in Imperial times—but never did the tomfoolery like me less. Muggy weather, miserable Carnival. No showers of *confetti*, no procession of the *bœuf gras* even. Here and there the orchestras of the theatres, clad in the cast-off finery of the supernumeraries thereof, parade the streets, and make dissonance with their instruments. Very German-bandish this dissonance sounds, with a variety of horror thrown in liberally in the shape of tambourines and triangles. One corps of mumming musicians is dressed as Zouaves; another might be directors of a Funeral Company, so sad their garments; a third is got up in a costume semi-nightshirt, semi-dressing-gown; all send out agents to tout for *backsheesh*. That is their great point of resemblance. The masquers are few in the streets, and, such as they are, wear their motley as if for pay, not for pastime. They are of the usual order, Pierrots, Polichinelles, and cavaliers, with no wigs, with powdered wigs, and with curly wigs, and with vizors hideous or ghastly, or simply droll and grotesque. Among the latter are some which might have been designed by Dykwnkyn for a Drury Lane pantomime; but the individual who carried off the palm of burlesque was an equestrian I met in the Plaza Mayor, looking like one of the men in armour of a Lord Mayor's show with bonneted head-gear, astride of a pot-bellied Clydesdale. Perhaps he may have been caricaturing "the ingenious gentleman" of La Mancha. My most grateful anticipation of Spain was, that it was behind the age, and was in no hurry to overtake it. But this did not hold good in Madrid, and dear womankind with the tiny feet was the culprit. She disfigured herself at that epoch with an enormous bustle on which a Barbary ape might conveniently rehearse a bolero. Well, we have had our Grecian bends, our crinolines and crinolettes, our pull-backs and Piccadilly limps. Fashion spells despot everywhere, and dear womankind will cheerfully obey its dictates, even though she have to blur her cheeks with patches, distort her spine, or tightlace herself into consumption.

In the afternoon a long procession of carriages (mostly hired) traverses the Calle de Alcalá and the promenade to the left of the fountain where Cybele is sculptured driving a pair of meekest ox-like lions; the folk in the carriages are not wildly joyous in their dissipation, nor are the horses that draw them restive with excitement. Everything is dull, consequently respectable; orderly, consequently dreary. The Foresters' *fête* at the Crystal Palace is more hilarious. No shafts of delicate raillery are shot by cherry lips; no peal of silvery laughter rings out. The Carnival is "stale, flat, and unprofitable," except to those mumming musicians who have paid sixteen shillings for the license to beg during the three mock-mirthful days. I survey the scene from a window in the Paseo de Recoletos, and get all my enjoyment out of the cynical remarks of a monstrously fine Burgundian lady, who criticises the dresses of her Spanish sisters as they glide by. The dresses are very tasteless, but the Frenchwoman's remarks are very ill-natured, and ill-nature is gratifying when your neighbour is its object. A friend enters and claps me on the back.

"Do you know, old fellow, that that stormy petrel of the Revolution, Cluseret of the Commune, is said to be in Madrid?"

"Never! What brings him here?"

"*Said* to be, was my expression," he added. "As a fact, I don't believe he is here, but they take you for him. That is how the tale of his arrival has got into the papers."

The Burgundian lady turns. "Cluseret!" she ejaculates; "absurd! I have seen Cluseret; he is much taller and much handsomer than this gentleman!"

I bowed to hide my face, which was what Mr. Whistler might have called a symphony in black and red, frown and blush. I have since thought what a caustic retort I might have made if I had said politely, "And, it is to be hoped, much more well-bred." But I said nothing, for the same reason that Dr. Johnson gave once to Boswell—"I had nothing ready, sir."

The panorama underneath is duller now; occasionally a foolish horseman canters by, covered as to his person and his charger's quarters with a flowing roquelaure of sheeny green satin; or a black-haired damsel trips it by, with features concealed by sky-blue mask, and proportions by an outer vesture of a painfully bright gamboge colour. I wonder is her hair her own, and are her eyes black. Most likely they are—night eyes are the rule here—the fair (that is the dark) sex are all going to purgatory if the French couplet be authority:—

"Les yeux noirs

Vont au purgatoire."

Again fanciful reflection is broken in upon by the thrumming of guitars, the shrill squeak of fifes, and the eternal whirr and jingle of the tambourines and triangles, and I descend and make my way through the fast-thickening crowds to my hotel. There, where the company, like the waiters, is polyglot; where a noble, white-bearded English gentleman is sandwiched between a little German professor and a Diputado to the Congress, where French journalists sit by young American exquisites, who are picking up notions in Europe, and mere tourists who have come to "do" Spain in thirteen days are listening to the experiences of a mining engineer from the West Riding of Yorkshire, who has been in the country for thirteen years; the gossip, unlike the fun without, is fast and furious. But as it is all of politics, and I gave the reader a dose of that in the last chapter and may have to repeat it anon, I turn to the windows and scan the ever-animated, always-varying picture on the Puerta del Sol. Ladies in veils white and black, as of Genoa and Milan respectively, pass and re-pass, gilt missals in their hands. They will be at the masked balls to-night, for this, as I have said already, is the home of paradox, where the announcement of the church in which the Quarant'ore, or Forty-hours' Exposition of the Sacrament, is being held, is printed in the same column with the theatrical advertisements. Over the way stand a group in the national "capa." Why do they not wear slouched and plumed beavers? To me a chimney-pot hat surmounting a cloak is as dire an outrage on poetic association as a Venetian bravo with a quizzing-glass. It offends the sense of fitness. What if the Madrileños were to take to the Ulster-coat? It would make a capital Carnival disguise at all events. But the cloak, is it not mysterious, brigandish—tragic, if you will? Mark that loosely-built, tawny man of dare-devil aspect on the edge, bending intently towards the excited speaker in the middle. Something has discomposed him, for his cheeks purple. There is an agitated flutter under the cloak, and its folds are flung back. You expect to be startled by the blade of a stiletto, and out comes a soiled pocket-handkerchief! It is as if Jupiter Tonans were to threaten a thunderbolt and compromise with a sneeze.

The third day of the Carnival, Shrove Tuesday, was all that could be desired, sunny, sprightly, bustling. The streets palpitated with merrymakers walking, riding, or driving, most of them handsomely dressed; the music—good, bad, and indifferent—was unceasing; the legions of roysterers attired themselves in every conceivable vagary of costume, even to the cheap resource of a chintz dressing-gown. They were cheerful, but in a business-like matter-of-fact way, and as they promenaded twirled corncrakes, jingled tin cans, and tootled horns. Few women disgraced themselves by appearing in men's clothes. Madrid is more continent than Paris; and, to its credit be it recorded, there was neither drunkenness nor horse-play. In the afternoon the scene in the Prado was kaleidoscopic in variety and beauty and motion; it had in it the gay element of the true Carnival, and those who had held aloof before or had been deterred from sharing in the *fête* by the inauspicious natural weather or by nervousness owing to the unsettled condition of the political weather, came out fresh, frolicsome, and bent on making up for lost time. Some of the dresses were luxurious, and triumphantly bore the test of sunshine, which is inexorable for what is worn or seedy or imitation. And yet there seldom was a time to which the stereotyped figure of speech about dancing on a volcano more strikingly applied. Electricity was in the air; the troops were under arms; the Deputies were consulting under the protection or the threat (as the balance of feeling might incline) of canister-stuffed cannon, and it was quite within the range of the possible that before nightfall the cavalry might be fetlock deep in blood, and the carnage of the Dos de Mayo be repeated— a worse carnage, for the Spaniards who fell then were patriots slain gloriously fighting against the foreigner, and now they would be Spaniards killed by brothers.

The stream of pleasure was in its full force and flow when a strange murmur followed by a succession of slight screams arrested the attention of the merrymakers. Faces were turned inquiringly towards the point whence the sounds came; the faces grew serious as a carriage was noticed breaking from the ranks and driving smartly down a side-street, they were overspread with alarm as other carriages filed off, and then, quick as a cloud overcasts the sun, a curtain of gloom fell upon the moving multitude. There was a halt as if by general consent, a dead silence, a thrill of trepidation, and a rapid rush and scurry hither and thither to shelter. Trailing skirts were caught up, vizors were thrown aside, grey-bearded patriarchs tore off their wigs and spectacles, the fiddling and singing came to an abrupt ending, and were replaced by curses and shrieks; all order and courtesy were cast to the four winds of heaven. It was a perfect tragi-comedy; a mixture of the terrible, the risible, the ominous, the rococo. I never saw transformation so sharp. It was as if there was no room for any less ignoble feeling in the lately jocose, bantering throngs than self-preservation. Drivers lashed their horses and mules and galloped off furiously; equestrians careered towards all points of the compass; those on foot bolted into every hall-way that stood ajar, or disappeared down the nearest openings; shrubs and flowers were trampled upon, and in a span shorter than it takes to recount it, the avenue of the Prado was a desert. It was fierce wholesale scamper and stampede. The roadway and parks were strewn with fans, masks, pocket-handkerchiefs, gloves and slippers; the entire company of masquerading Arabs, Prussian officers, Morris dancers, Inquisitors, and troubadours had taken incontinent flight, most of them breathless and white; the ladies in their varied characters of gipsies, grisettes, Galician nurses, and Court coquettes had all scudded off in such a dismayed flutter that they had forgotten to swoon, and forfeited the finest of opportunities of breaking into hysterics. They were really frightened. I sought refuge (from what I knew not, whether earthquake, hurricane or revolution) in a thick clump of bushes at the side of the Paseo, where I stumbled over a panting make-believe toreador, and a curious wire-woven article of ladies' dress, which latter I appropriated as trophy. By-and-by, as no fresh cry of alarm was raised, the bull-fighter crawled out, and I took heart of grace to return to the centre of the town, where I learned that the scare was groundless. It had its origin in the glitter of the bayonets of some soldiers returning from their duties at the Palace of the Congress. Madrid was timid as a sick girl. It struck me that if there had been genuine cause for the panic, and that a charge had been made or a volley with lead fired, there would have been unequalled scope for a picture of the type of Gérôme's "Duel after the Bal Masqué," but on a more liberal scale—Polichinelle pierced by a bayonet-thrust, the floured face of Pierrot streaked with blood, and poor Jack Pudding sprawling in the death-agonies in the gutter.

The festivities were prolonged to the small hours of the night, or rather of the morning, none the less vigorously for the passing fear-spasm in the Prado; the masked balls at the theatres were packed with guests who enjoyed themselves, or fancied they did, which is as much as one can reasonably expect in this mundane sphere sometimes.

The "Marseillaise" from a vibrating brass band might be heard, nay almost felt, crashing through the glass-doors and bursting in a cataract of sound through the drapery at the entrances of the café on the ground-floor of the Fonda de Paris at the hour when honest burgesses should be *tête-à-tête* with the pillow.

On Ash Wednesday, which rose rainily, there was an augmentation in the average of headaches, and a rise in the rates for apothecary's stuff. The pious revellers went (with an interval for washing and change of clothes) from the ball-room to the churches to receive the ashes. "Remember, man, thou art but dust, and unto dust thou shalt return," says the priest, and smears their foreheads with the cinders of last year's palm-branches. Another custom, peculiar to the date, the "entierro de la sardina," was duly observed by those wicked rogues, the non-pious revellers. The sardina is not the fish, but a portion of the intestines of a pig, which is laid to earth with pseudo-lamentation in token of *carne vale*, farewell to flesh-meat for forty days. With a lugubrious affectation of grief the funeral pageant passed. It was very profane—an undissembled mockery of a religious procession. A banner striped pink and yellow and inscribed "á los Cubanos" was carried in front by a fellow in West Indian negro dress with blackened face. Next came a troop of blackened acolytes, two by two, and then a canopy such as is borne over the Host, which canopy was held in travesty of homage over a beer-keg. A sacrilegious choir, chanting a parody of a Gregorian hymn, paced behind, and a gigantic blackguard, the *serpent du village*, supplied a droning accompaniment from a bassoon. A blackened high-priest, with a conical black hat and a cope bee-barred black and yellow, closed the burlesque train and made believe to read a mass-book through his pantomimic goggles. There was an attendant who rang a funeral bell, another who tapped a muffled drum, and a third who swung right under the nostrils of the onlookers a censer containing ground resin made vile to the smell by some fetid compound. Occasionally the profane rascals halted for a pull at a goat-skin of wine.

There are some queer customs, the undeniable relics of paganism, in Spain. On Christmas-eve the streets are paraded by men rattling pots, just as the Romans used to celebrate the row that was made in Olympus to hide the birth of Jupiter from Saturn. In the Basque provinces they honour the Virgin Mary under the name of Astarte, a clear loan from the worship of Venus. As I am treating of queer customs, it is worth chronicling that the Republicans entered the churches as soon as their favourite Government was proclaimed and frantically rang the bells. A Bishop took care to exorcise the Republican demon next day by carefully sprinkling the bells with holy-water.

For all the Lent, the treacherous and trying weather, the wars and rumours of wars, Madrid enjoyed herself, ate, drank and made merry, flirted and gambled. The Opera, a cosy well-frequented resort of the fashionable set, was open, and gave the *Creation* and *L'Africaine*, and the usual repertory of musical masterpieces of which I plead profound technical ignorance redeemed by passionate fondness. The soprano was that plump goddess with the dimpled double chin, fair-haired Marie Sass. The orchestra was one of the finest I had ever heard, and the chorus in personal appearance one of the ugliest I had ever seen, and that, I can assure the reader, is saying much. The Zarzuela, a play-house devoted to opera-bouffe—the sacred lamp of burlesque was not trimmed—presented "Golden Dreams," a beautiful piece with plot and fun not cumbered with that scenic sumptuousness which is trying to edge acting ability off the boards elsewhere.

The respectable theatres in Madrid shut their doors on the Fridays in Lent, and respectable theatre-goers remain at home. It is not the correct thing to be seen pleasure-hunting on a day of mortification and white meats. But actors must live, as well as in London. Those who are connected with high-priced houses and are decently paid can afford to lose one night in the week. But there are poorer followers of the Thespian art who are in very bad case indeed, owing to this tribute to religious scruple. If we are to be virtuous, well and good: but let us be virtuous in earnest. We have bull-fights on the Sundays in Lent. Why may we not enjoy the singing of Marie Sass in *Norma* on a Lenten Friday? This thin distinction between what is right and what is not—so thin that men of the cold north cannot make it out—comes under the category of those indigenous peculiarities which surpass all understanding. Anyhow, it presses rather heavily on the humble votaries of the sock and buskin who are attached to the middle-class houses, and who are docked of one night's salary in every week of the seven in the penitential season, in order that the proprieties of a public which is not particular to a shade as to how it observes the Sabbath may be respected. The low theatres—the Romea, where the Republic is glorified; the Alhambra, where heels are kicked up and lewd songs are rolled forth; the Capellanes, where monks and nuns are caricatured, have reason on their side, at all events. They dare to be logical in their contempt for the Church, and keep open all the year round, on Friday as on Sunday, in the time of fasting as of feasting.

The Teatro Martin is not a low theatre nor yet is it a high-priced one. The actors there are not rich, but the audience has some pretensions to delicacy of taste. What is the lessee of the Martin to do during the Lent? To rob his treasury of one night's receipts and cheat his patrons of one night's enjoyment? That would be the last crime any spirited and enterprising lessee would dream of committing—if he could avoid it. From this dilemma the gentleman of the Teatro Martin has discovered an escape. He opens his house on Fridays, but he converts it into a temple; he reconciles amusement with religion; he produces a Passion Play! I went to see it for the special reason that it was my privilege once to describe the Passion Play in the Bavarian Highlands, and I was anxious to compare one representation with the other, and, if possible, to renew my emotions of the past.

The house was tolerably full, except the boxes, which were unoccupied, save one by a sedate family party. Devout folk of the Latin race are famous for the interest they take in the spectacular. They admire the pomps of religion; and this Passion Play, which was almost a function, had evidently brought many to the theatre who are seldom seen there on ordinary occasions. I thought I could detect a pious bearing in the pittites. The well-to-do persons—male and female—who sat patiently on the mouldy benches looked serious, as if they had come to assist at a sacrifice. There were old ladies there, I could almost take my word, who are more often to be encountered, with morocco-bound prayer-books in their shrivelled hands, creeping to early service. The gallery was packed, and the gods, for gods, were gentlemanlike. There was nothing in the aspect of the house meriting description—it was roomy, ill-lit, full of draughts and dust—one of those houses we know so well. The scene-painter, if the act-drop was a fair sample of his powers, was a victim to colour-blindness; the orchestra showed a Republican freedom in its scorn for the trammels of time and tune; but the prompter in his hooded box, full in the middle of the range of footlights, was the feature of the show. He had a very distinct voice—so distinct was it that every sentence he directed to the actors rebounded from the flats, came back in sibilant echo, and ascended to the gods. I have no intention of giving an analysis of the piece; to speak the sad truth, it did not come up to my expectations. Ober-Ammergau spoiled me for exhibitions of the kind. I could not screw up my enthusiasm, tried I ever so hard. That which charmed in Bavaria had no charm in Spain. The stately panorama which was put before the awe-struck spectator in that valley of the Ammer was not visible here. The blue sky overhead and the eternal hills in sight above the walls of the simple wooden structure; the music so tender and solemn; the clear-browed peasants losing their identity in the fervid rendering of their parts; the enraptured attention of the auditory, whose lips moved in prayer sometimes, and whose eyes sometimes brimmed with tears, as if the scenes they watched were real—those were things to be remembered. They were the points that helped to make an impression in Bavaria, that dispelled prejudice and replaced it with a pleased satisfaction which insensibly swelled to admiration; but they were wanting in this stuffy play-house. No illusion was possible. One never lost the consciousness that he was looking on at a stage-play acted for money by indifferent stage-players. There was a smell of paint and tobacco-smoke about. Then there was the voice of that irrepressible prompter, the shaven faces of the hungry supernumeraries who played the Roman soldiers, the gas-rakes, the shaky wings, the mark of the trap-doors from which devils with a family likeness to the imps of pantomime spring up to-night, and the statue of the Commander may emerge to-morrow night, the scenes that would not run smoothly in the grooves, and the stiff stereotyped exits and entrances. Everything was of the stage, stagey. One could not get rid of the notion that Caiaphas had dined on puchero with its flavour heightened by garlic. It was very palpable that the Apostle Peter wore a wig and a beard of tow. Mary Magdalen had an air of operatic resignation, and was troubled with the arrangement of her drapery. There was a layer of pearl-powder on the Virgin's cheeks.

I shall not bore the reader with an essay on mysteries and miracle-plays; neither, as I have said, shall I attempt to analyse this sacred drama, in seven acts, of "The Passion and Death of Jesus;" but I shall take the liberty of giving an epitome of some notes, pencilled on the spot, in the intervals of interruption by that loud prompter. The *Pasion y Muerte de Jesus* (that is the Spanish title) is written by Don Enrique Zumel, who appears to have fathered as many pieces as Lope de Vega, but whose pieces are not quite so well known. It was brought out for the first time in this self-same Teatro Martin on the 3rd of March, 1871. It is in verse, and has some literary merit. In the main incidents it resembles the Bavarian play, which does not deviate noticeably from the Bible narrative. It is unnecessary, therefore, to go over the incidents of its various acts. The Greek chorus to be remarked at Ober-Ammergau is absent. The tableaux from the Old Testament prefiguring events in the New are absent also. The first Act opens with a dialogue between Magdalen and some women of Jerusalem. The Saviour, with the Apostles, enters on the scene almost immediately after. Magdalen's garments are rich with spangles; her mantle is scarlet; she has flowers in her luxuriant tresses, and looks a vain creature. The Saviour is personified by an actor with a singular likeness to Joseph Mayer, the Bavarian Christus. Pale, clean-chiselled face, long black locks smoothed over, downcast eyes, a meek demeanour generally—the characteristics are identical. The voice of this man, who essayed so awful a *rôle*, was low and sweet; and, to give him his due, he moved as if he was filled with respect for his dangerous part. The Virgin comes on the scene in the same Act. She is clad in blue nun-like raiment. The people who filled up the background wore sandals, and had white towels, swathed in folds like those of the turban, round their raven-black hair. The entry into Jerusalem was shown, the Saviour being mounted on a white ass. The orchestra here woke up, and played a joyous strain to a chorus commencing—

"Con palmas y oliva

Y alegre cantar

Y pintados florea

De lindos colores

Hijas de Judá

Llegad! Llegad!"

and terminating with a hosannah to the Redeemer. The only anachronisms in dress that impressed me in this first Act were a silk net with which one young person of Jerusalem confined her rebellious hair, and a strip of black velvet which another had fastened round her throat, bringing out the whiteness of her skin by contrast. In the second Act Caiaphas speaks of Jesus as the fomenter of a "thousand conflicts between Church and State." The Last Supper is pictured after Leonardo da Vinci, and Judas comes into relief, a sullen scowler, who overdoes his part thus early. In the garden scene in the third Act the figure of Jesus in prayer is shown with a ray of *luz Dumont*, the lime-light of our London stage, playing upon it! I left my seat after this, and loitered outside till the Crucifixion scene was on. At Ammergau it was appallingly impressive; here it was sensational purely. The drama wound up with the bursting open of the sepulchre. I came away free from any desire to witness Don Enrique Zumel's production again. Without absolutely shocking one's feelings on a subject which should be sacred and approached reverently, if at all, his Passion Play offended fine taste throughout because of the obtrusive staginess of its action, get-up, and surroundings. Still the actors were occasionally applauded, and the audience left in a contented mood.

But the provisional rulers took care that those under their guardianship should have stronger pabulum than spoon-meat.

Napoleon I., unless the tale be a legend, used to order a new coat of gilding to be laid on the dome of the Invalides when the people of Paris chafed under his tyranny. That gave them something to talk about—supplied a sensation of twenty-four hours. The Spanish Republican governors are working on the same principle. *Panes et circenses* was the charter of the Roman plebs, "pan y toros" is that of the plebs of Madrid. I do not know how it is with the bread, but the rulers let the lieges have bulls galore to occupy their minds. There are grand corridas for professionals and amateurs. Nor is bull-fighting the only pastime provided for the populace; cock-fighting, with game-birds from the Canary Islands, is also carried on every Sunday morning in a pit constructed for the purpose, mains are scientifically fought, and money is prodigally squandered. All countries have their peculiarities. In some, people go racing on the Lord's Day; in others they are content with getting drunk in the bosoms of their families.

NOTE BY MY VERY LEARNED AND AMIABLE ACCOMPLICE, DR. DANN.—That great writer on Spanish folk-lore, Mesonero Romanos, better known as "El curioso parlante," who flourished some fifty years since, seems utterly ignorant of the record of the "entierro." His account only goes to show that Spain is the most conservative country of Europe. A huge "sardina" placed on the top of a bier is carried by a number of fellows in carnival costume, each of them having on his head a cone of immense height, somewhat resembling the dunce's cap that was formerly such a usual thing in English village-schools. In front, and at the back of the procession, appears a crowd of young men and of girls from the slums of Southern Madrid, in three groups, called "coros," or choirs. There is the "coro de mancebos," or young men's choir; the "coro de doncellas," or girls' choir; and the "coro de inocentes," or innocents' choir. The *locus in quo* is that part of the south of the

Spanish capital which extends from the Vistillas de San Francisco to the Church of San Lorenzo; for, in contradistinction to Paris, the South of Madrid is almost exclusively inhabited by what M. Gambetta used to call the new social strata, while Mr. Bright spoke of them many years ago as the *residuum*. In connection with the sardina, and rising on the same coffin, a figure of "Uncle Marcos" is carried, somewhat similar in form to the stuffed Guy Fawkeses which are carried about in the streets of London on the 5th of November. When the procession has reached the Puente Toledana, the figure of Uncle Marcos is burnt on a funeral pile, and the sardina is buried in a ditch prepared on purpose. While all this is going on, songs intended to be parodies of the Catholic Church hymns and canticles are chanted by the accompanying choirs, and altogether the performance is, for all practical purposes, a parody of the Church processions so frequent in Spain and all Southern countries. When it is all over, a good many of the actors indulge in libations. Not unfrequently the burial of the sardina is followed by a free fight, and half a dozen dead or wounded are the outcome of the battle. Disgusting as the whole performance may appear, more especially the blasphemous simulacre of religious worship, it must be admitted in palliation that the very idea of mocking the rites of the Catholic, Apostolic and Roman Church never so much as enters the minds of the performers, who would repudiate with the utmost indignation the notion of intentionally placing themselves outside the pale of the Church, and violating the "buenas costumbres" by what they are doing.

CHAPTER VIII.

Another Chat with Mentor—A Startling Solution of the Spanish Question—The Penalties of Popularity—The Republic another Saturn—The New Civil Governor—The Government Bill—Outside the Palace of the Congress—Providential Rain—Wild Rumours—Federal Threats—The Five Civil Guards—Inside the Chamber—The Great Debate—The Two Reports—Compromise—Minor Speechmakers—A Pickwickian Contention—The Division—Victory for the Ministry—The Five Civil Guards Trot to Stables.

ON the morning of March 8th, I met my Anglo-Spanish Mentor in the reading-room of the hotel. To my usual inquiry as to the condition of health of the Republic, he replied that he thought we were nearing the critical point.

"There is a cataclysm impending," he said. "We have got beyond the stage of changing the names of streets and substituting the Hymn of Riego for the Royal March. Everybody agrees that a *coup d'état* is necessary, and may be imminent; we want an intelligent despotism—but the despot must always be a man of our own party. There is the hitch. Castelar probably may have some amiable hobby, like Lamartine, of 'employment for adults and education for the young.' Whatever be the sequel of the trial of strength, I hope we may have a strong administration, not one like the present, where the Minister of Grace and Justice is all grace and no justice.

"Do you know," he added, after a pause, "I have an idea as to the solution of this Spanish question?"

"What is it, pray?"

"SELL SPAIN TO ENGLAND!"

I roared with derisive laughter.

"I am serious," he continued. "This is the age of arbitration. Why not of colossal international barter? We could rule the country as we rule India, set Sikh against Hindoo, and play off Ghoorka against both."

"You do not reckon with Spanish pride," I said.

"Bah! The pride that lowered itself to the acceptance of foreign royalty might condescend to pocket foreign gold."

"When Pedro brought me my chocolate this morning he told me there had been demonstrations in some of the lower quarters."

"Yes; but they are easily accounted for. The populace do not see the impracticable promises of the Republicans realized, and are impatient for the millennium of liberty, equality, and fraternity, with no work and lots to eat superadded. But the demonstration was very trivial, it limited itself to the sticking of a red flag in front of a hall-door. There are wicked slanderers who say that Figueras had something to do with it, and passed the word that the 'people' should bring an outward pressure to bear upon his brethren of the Assembly, so that he might get rid of some of his ungrateful colleagues by the argument, 'See, you are impossible, the people won't have you; better for the sake of order leave, that you may avoid the humility of being sent away.'"

"Surely," I expostulated, "Señor Figueras would not descend to such a base trick of democracy!"

"My innocent friend," said Mentor, "once a man binds himself to what is falsely called the 'people' he has to put up with much inconvenience, swallow his pride, and humour his exacting pet. Figueras knows this already; he has been stopped by groups in the streets at various times, and obliged to amuse them by small harangues, the same as if he were a Punch-and-Judy showman, making his 'pitch' for ha'pence."

"Unpleasant situation," I remarked. "He must weary of that soon."

"Most likely his admirers will weary of him—and then," said Mentor, with a chuckle—"then for a spell of chaos. The Republic, like Saturn, has an ugly propensity for devouring its offspring. The mob fondles Republicanism as its exclusive property, spreads palm-branches under the feet of its prophets one week and stones them the next. Castelar, Figueras, Pi y Margall, are the prophets to-day; they will be victimised in the end. To them will succeed men more violent, who will make larger promises, and then, finally, will spring up a strong reaction and a return to something old-fashioned and stable."

Mentor was a thorough-paced Conservative and a pessimist into the bargain. In order to draw him out I pleaded that the Government was doing its best to conciliate all parties. For instance, it had appointed Estévanez, Civil Governor of Madrid.

"Aye," said Mentor, "another evidence of the truth of what I advance. That was done to please the Intransigentes. Estévanez is beloved of the Reds, and took to the hills a few months ago in assertion of Federal Republican principles. He held the rocky mountain pass of Despeñar Perros in Andalusia, at the head of a handful of men, but he boasts that he neither destroyed railways nor cut telegraphic wires, and holds certificates to that effect from the railway companies and the Government. He is an old soldier, a man of energy, and his influence with his party in this province is paramount. If the Constituent Cortes proclaim a moderate or a united Republic he may make himself obstructive. But I must bid you good-day; I am off for my constitutional in the Botanical Gardens."

The reference to the Constituent Cortes reminded me that this was the date appointed for the consideration of the Government Bill for their election, introduced into Congress on the night of the 4th of March. This Bill consisted of eight articles, the most important of which were that the elections should take place on the 10th of April and three following days, and the meeting on the 1st of May; that all Spaniards above the age of twenty should have votes; and that on the suspension of the session of the existing Cortes a permanent committee from their members, with consultative functions, should be appointed for the interregnum. It was felt that this was throwing down the glove, and the lines were now marshalling for the tug of war. The Radicals are disquieted. They know that if they go to the country not one-third of them will be returned, for the reason that whoever holds the Ministry of the Gobernacion, or Interior, in this paradise of universal suffrage can return the nominees of his party, and determine their majorities with mathematical certainty. Ministers act illegally in the article which provides that men of twenty may vote. The young men are the main strength of Republicanism everywhere, and this article at a single arbitrary scratch of the pen adds half a million electors to the rolls. Hitherto the right of voting was restricted to males who had attained twenty-five years. The Radicals object to this sweeping alteration in the law, made with the distinct object of defeating their chances; and the hatred of those half-million of young men thus sought to be enfranchised by the new Republic will be acquired to the Radicals from the very fact of their opposition.

When the hour for opening the Congress came, the building looked more like a barrack than a House of Parliament. A grim Guardia Civil, in a three-cornered hat, stood sentry, with fixed bayonet, at the side-door in the Calle de Turco, by which the Deputies enter. At every window men in uniform were to be seen; officers with jangling scabbards moved about the lobbies and ante-rooms, instead of the usual moody, sallow, shabby crowd of taciturn waiters on Providence, muffled in mantles and hidden in smoke, who hang about for hours, and occasionally pass mysterious slips of paper by the liveried and silver-laced ushers to Señor Don This or That within.

What can their business be? I often puzzle myself by asking. Have they claims on Government for ancestral property gone down in the Armada? Are they pretenders to the succession in a licence to sell tobacco and salt in Minorca? Or are they simply intriguing for a ticket to the House? The problem waits for solution.

They are not here to-day. In their places are the soldiers who watch over the safety of the representatives of the people. Luckily it is wet, and the crowds outside cower and huddle under a camp of umbrellas. Your persistent drizzle is a terrible enemy to revolution. There is nothing like it for putting a damper on noisy out-of-door agitation. But the occasion is a great one, and though the clouds seem to have been transformed into tanks with bottoms pepper-castored with leaks, and never tire of the weary drip-drip, the citizens of Madrid bravely affront the weather and collect on the sloppy approaches to the Palace of the Congress to discuss the affairs of the commonwealth. They look resolute enough to go under a shower-bath in the interest of their country. Patiently they stand, with knit brows, their soaked mantles clinging to their persons, while the Deputies drive or walk up, and enter to take part in the important discussion at hand—the discussion which is to decide whether there are to be barricades in Madrid and in all the great cities, and some widows the more in Spain within four-and-twenty hours.

Denser grow the throngs and livelier the excitement, for all the rain. Reports the most eccentric and alarming are bandied about. The people have burned down the churches in Malaga; but Malagueño, "as everybody knows," remarks a French journalist, "is the synonym for *méchant.*" In another knot a rumour circulates that a meeting of Radicals had been held the evening previous, at which the German, Austrian, and Italian ambassadors were present, and that they spoke of the necessity of a joint intervention to assist in the restoration of peace. This senseless rumour was believed by some fools, and the Radicals who were supposed to be ready to open the door to the foreigner were cursed and hissed, or howled at, as they stepped into the Palace. Word passes that the Intransigentes are in arms in the lower quarters of the town, and have taken up "strategic points" in view of any emergency that may arise. If the Government is beaten they mean to raise the red flag, to occupy the theatres as they did once before, to turn the Plaza Santa Ana and the Plazuela de Anton Martin into head-quarters, and, if necessary, to march on the Parliament-house and make an example of those traitorous Radicals who would betray the people and bring back the Monarchy. Law-fearing Madrid is in a state of wan terror, and thanks Providence for that thrice-blessed rain. The men who compose the noisy groups belong to the lower classes; they are not very numerous, but they are very determined. The active demonstration is confined to a nucleus of some one hundred and fifty persons. Delegates occasionally arrive from distant parts of the town, whisper to comrades in the mob, and depart. It is known that the troops are confined to barracks, that a hundred picked men of the Guardia Civil have reinforced the garrison of the Palace of Congress, and that Señor Martos has not quitted it since the previous night.

Try and realise to yourself a crowd from Clerkenwell Green surging and yelling angrily in the open space before Westminster Hall, a battalion of the Coldstreams keeping watch and ward on the faithful Commons, and Mr. Speaker, for reasons of personal security, compelled to have a shakedown in the House!

At half-past three o'clock the flag is run up to the head of the staff on the roof, but it droops limp and woebegone in the wet. The Assembly is in session. The waiting crowds increase; the windows commanding a view of the Palace are filled, and the pavements of the streets contiguous are black with anxious loiterers, in spite of the detestable weather. News of what is going on inside the Chamber escapes by driblets; as soon as a Deputy or a reporter comes out he is button-holed and interviewed.

"The Radicals hold firm," says one, and there is a howl of rage, and the chattering *flâneurs*, who linger on the pavement at a safe distance, stir their heels with a rare unity of sentiment. "Devil take the hindmost!" is the motto of these dignified burgesses of Madrid when a cry of danger is raised; bang go the shutters against the shop-windows in a jiffy.

At one period the attitude of the crowd immediately opposite the entrance of the Palace boded ill; cries of "Viva la República Federal!" and "Death to the Radicals!" were raised, and Señor Estévanez, the Civil Governor of Madrid, was obliged to come out and speak to his pet lambs, and pacify them with the assurance that the Federal Republic was safe. Five mounted Civil Guards took up their stations at the mouth of the Calle de Turco after this, and stood there silent, statue-like, with drawn swords in their gauntleted grip, until day had melted into twilight, and twilight into night. These five cavaliers, in their heavy cloaks, blacker than the darkness around, had really something supernatural in their grisly quietude as they rested stock-still in their saddles. Their mission was ominous of evil; they were there an ugly index of what was feared. Had they found it necessary to clap spur to their horses and plunge upon the mob, I would not have given much for their lives. Those five "lost sentinels" were sure to have been picked off before their comrades on foot could have sallied from the adjacent building to their rescue. Sinister-looking fellows, in jackets and fur caps, with rifles slung across their shoulders, were not ensconced in the street-corners in easy range without a purpose.

The scene inside the Chamber gave equal token that a question of vital interest was being debated. The gallery assigned to the public was crammed as closely as the pit of Drury Lane on Boxing Night; the press gallery ran over with reporters; every seat available was full but those reserved for the ambassadors. Their seats were empty; not even the war-worn figure of General Sickles was to be distinguished. Cristinos Martos, looking anxious but firm, was in the presidential chair; and the halberdiers in purple and gold, with their heavy silver maces and nodding white plumes, occupied their accustomed places to the right and left.

The President rings his bell for business. The first operation is to read the minutes of the previous sitting, which are approved. Then one of those obstructive members to be encountered in every legislative assembly—be it

Reichsrath, Rigsdag, Skupstina, or Storthing—rises to take his little innings on some petty topic that concerns none beyond his own small circle. He is quickly bowled out, and the order of the day is arrived at—that for which we are all waiting, that which makes this one of the most serious and important sittings since the abdication of the King. The reading of the reports of the committee was first proceeded with, that of the majority taking precedence. This document was rather long, but may be summarised into a lament that the Government intended to make the permanent committee a purely consultative body; a declaration that the time was unsuitable for an election, civil war being actually carried on in Spain; and a protest that the clause establishing twenty as the age from which the privilege of voting dated was "an abuse and an irregularity." It concluded with a project of law, in a single article, binding the Assembly to convoke the Cortes whenever it considered the condition of the country such as to guarantee freedom of suffrage and the interests of the Republic.

Primo de Rivero's report was then read. He based it on the conviction that the transitory period should be closed in the interest of domestic order, and that the Constituent Cortes would be the true representation of the national will. To effect conciliation, he would submit a bill fixing May 10th as the period of election, June 1st as that of the meeting of the Cortes, and twenty-one as the age at which Spaniards should have power to exercise electoral rights.

The consideration of the report of the minority, which was looked on as an amendment, came first.

The Chief of the Executive Power, Figueras, himself opened the discussion. The Government had presented a bill so framed that they hoped it would satisfy the divers aspirations of the Assembly. They thought they could go no further, but since Primo de Rivero had seen fit to draw up his conciliatory report they had resolved to modify their primitive proposition in certain particulars, such as the definition of the faculties of the permanent committee and the date of the elections. But that was the extreme limit of compromise. They would stand or fall by the vote about to be given. If the Chamber gave them its support they would proceed with the rude task of administration, and they were resolved firmly to sustain order, military discipline, and the majesty of the law. Here Señor Figueras branched off into a schoolboy digression as to what the law was, and how it should be administered. Coming to the real point, he said if Primo de Rivero's bill were rejected, the Cabinet would hand in its resignation, and would ask the representatives to name its successors on the spot, for in those critical moments a solution of continuity in power would be attended with grave risks.

Señor Guardia then rose to deny that the existing Chamber had fulfilled its mission, and that the opportune time had arrived for the election of another. The very Government itself had made avowal to that effect. Certain bills remained to be discussed and voted. Besides, had they not other duties of greater necessity? What was the state of the country? An armed absolutism prevailed in some provinces; Catalonia recognised no chiefs but those of the locality (here there were interruptions). In the cities of the South, the public forces had abandoned their arms to persons more or less authorised in some of them, and in others the partition of sacred property had been announced. In the heart of Castile and Andalusia the ayuntamientos had to resign in the presence of superior force. Under those circumstances no elections could be carried on with liberty. And, as if this were not sufficient, there was an article which added 400,000 electors to the register. This was an aggravation of difficulties when mistrust was supreme everywhere. The majority of the reporting committee (of which he formed part) believed that the initiative of a convocation of the Cortes should come, not from the Government, but from the Chamber. The destruction of the elements which were not represented in the Government was what was sought by this call for a new Chamber.

Primo de Rivero then explained his position, which was curious. He, a member of the Radical party, disagreed with his colleagues; but his motive was the salvation of the Republic. If his bill were not accepted, the disasters that would fall upon the country would be tremendous and immediate. This plump declaration created what is called "sensation." The General next reviewed the different solutions which offered themselves. A new Cabinet of Republicans of long standing was not to be thought of, and a mixed Cabinet would be a calamity. One other solution remained, the formation of a Cabinet from the Radical majority. With all respect he would ask, Did that majority possess the moral authority to raise the standard of Republicanism? Did they recollect that their former chief, Ruiz Zorilla, called them cowards because they were about to proclaim the Republic? He repudiated the accusation.

Here there was a row, which recalled to mind that famous one between Mr. Pickwick and Mr. Blotton, of Aldgate. Señor Juan Ramon Zorilla rose to defend his absent relative. After a call to order, and a palaver, during which Primo de Rivero explained that he was speaking merely of Señor Zorilla the politician, but that Señor Zorilla personally was all that was honourable and patriotic, the discussion flowed back into its proper channel.

The General frankly admitted that the Radicals lacked moral authority. "Now," he said, "we are Republicans, but a month ago we were Monarchists." He then related with an ingenuousness that was remarkable in a professed friend, all the faults his party had committed, and prophesied that if a Radical Cabinet were formed it would not last three days. Who knows what might occur? Interruptions punctuated the soldier's discourse, but he turned round and told those who did not like what he said, that prudence was better than valour when valour was stupid and made reckless exposure of lives. He wound up by asking the representatives to seek inspiration in their patriotism and love of liberty, and support his bill, which he confessed was his in spirit only, and had not been drawn up by him but by members of the Government.

These opening orations of the champions of the two parties in the committee, the majority of six, and the minority of one, give the pith of the arguments *pro* and *con*. Then followed talkee-talkee by obscurities—speechlets of the maundering school, habitual of nights in St. Stephen's, when wise men betake themselves to the terrace, and the stenographers yawn and chew their pencils. A Republican editor declared that the Republican press was all that was lovely, and a Deputy from Barcelona affirmed that the city by the Mediterranean was a model of tranquillity (why was there a loud "haw-haw" here?). One of the Zorilla family rose to defend his absent namesake a second time, and Señor Lopez, chairman of the reporting committee, asseverated that the Radicals had no yearning for office, that the Government should be satisfied with an Assembly so liberal and so much inclined to help it, and that if anarchy were to be the issue, the waters of the Jordan would not wash the men who ruled of the responsibility. Then Cristinos Martos descended from his tribune, and said he would accept any arrangement which would secure peace. The crisis had come. The question by which the Ministry had elected to stand or fall was put to the test, and exactly nineteen Radicals, less than a score out of over two hundred, voted in the opposition.

So the Republicans retain their seats and bloodshed is averted. The mercy is due, not to the goodness of the cause, nor to the persuasive pleadings of its advocates, but to the intimidation of the mob. The Radical majority were the judges, and the judges were cowed by the rabble of the streets and their spokesmen in the Chamber. The Radical majority had it in their power to put the Republicans off the coveted blue benches of the Treasury; but the Radical majority, feeling that there were no strong arms outside to back them, "caved in." That is the plain way of putting it. Five members out of every six in the house were Radicals, six out of seven of the sections of the house were Radical. Those sections, or standing committees, are drawn by lot on the first of every month, and all members must belong to one or other of them. Every bill that is presented must be referred to a committee composed of seven members, one selected by each section. Six of the members of the committee to report on the bill of dissolution presented by Señor Figueras were Radicals; one solitary member, General Primo de Rivero, recalled from fighting the Carlists in Guipúzcoa, favoured the Government. The Opposition stood to the Ministry as six to one. And the Opposition being thus strong, the Ministry had beaten it! The wonder ceases when it is recollected that the hands of the majority were tied; every plan was tried to influence them into not ousting the Ministry—coaxing and cajolery, appeals to their love of peace and country, and ultimately threats. As result, when it came to the "who shall?" they did not sustain the convictions they had openly expressed on all previous occasions. Peradventure this was patriotism, peradventure it was prudence.

The debate was over. It was ten o'clock. The crowd raised exultant shouts and dispersed to their homes, to the clubs, or to the coffee-houses, where there was soon a file-fire of hand-claps to summon the waiters and a Babel of voluble jabber. The five ghostly cavaliers outside the Palace of the Congress started to life, sheathed their sabres, caught up their bridles, and returned to their stables.

The Republic had been reprieved. What a sigh of relief San Isidro Labrador, patron of Madrid, must have heaved.

CHAPTER IX.

The Inventions of Don Fulano de Tal—Stopping a Train—"A Ver Fine Blaggar"—The Legend of Santa Cruz—Dodging a Warrant— Outlawed—Chased by Gendarmes—A Jack Sheppard Escape—The Cura becomes Cabecilla—Sleeping with an Eye Open—Exploits and Atrocities—Dilettante Carlists in London—The Combat of Monreal— Ibarreta's Relics—A Tale for the Marines—The Carlists Looking-up.

EVERY other day—every other hour, I might almost say—a new rumour was born in Madrid. These rumours were usually figments, always exaggerations. If one were to inquire into their origin Don Fulano de Tal, the Man in the Street, was certain to have assisted as *accoucheur*. Alas! truth in Spain is coyest of sparrows, and to be caught must have not a grain but a whole bushel of salt shaken over its tail. Don Carlos was always turning up somewhere like a bad shilling. Were he to be where he was said to be, he must have been a supernatural Don Carlos—must have inherited the seven-leagued boots of fairy tale, as his brother had the invisible cloak, for he was here, there, everywhere, and nowhere, at one and the same time. But wherever hovered the Pretender, or the "heir presumptuous," as a Spanish acquaintance, not well up in English as "she is spoke," persisted in calling him, or whatever he may have been doing, there could be no doubt that some of his followers were in the field and alarmingly active. On the 13th of March, the capital was furious at the official news that communication with France and the rest of Europe by the north had been cut. Vitoria was the limit of Spain now; beyond it was the troublous No Man's Land, where the legends of Manuel Santa Cruz and his desperadoes abounded. He it was who had ripped up the rails near Tolosa, and waited for the accident which was sure to occur when the first train travelling towards the frontier would arrive. Four inoffensive passengers were hurled into eternity. The excuse for the conduct of this minister of peace was that these trains carried troops. If the railway company would pay him a tribute and engage to carry no troops, Santa Cruz, who is accommodating, would let them pass freely. The company was willing, for these interruptions were killing the dividends, but the Government objected. In common justice to the more intelligent members of the party this soldier-priest disgraced, it should be admitted that they cursed him loudly and deeply. His conduct was bringing his order into disrepute. For instance, in Vitoria, near his own hunting-ground, when the Republic was proclaimed, the Civil Governor dropped a hint that it would be necessary to "exterminate the highwaymen of the black soutane." The priests of the town got so frightened that they did not dare to show themselves in the streets. But they were in no danger, though the merciless Manuel was doing what he could to make the priests' garb unpopular. A Carlist paper in Madrid, with some conscience left, had the honesty to say Manuel was not a credit to his cloth, and that Don Carlos did not approve of the many savage acts he had committed. Manuel sent the editor a letter, with his compliments, promising to teach him better manners than to speak ill of the absent when he came to Madrid! The general anticipation, based on a fond hope, was that if Manuel ever did come to Madrid, it would be strapped on a hurdle. But he had his admirers, nevertheless. My friend, the Duke de Fitzpepper, swore in his execrable execrating English that he was a "cottam ver fine blaggar—oh, ye-es! *tous qu'il y avait de plus crâne, mon cher!*" From one of these admirers who knew his family, I obtained an interesting epitome of his career.

Santa Cruz was born at Elduayen in Guipúzcoa in 1842. An aged uncle gave him some lessons in Latin, and placed him in an ecclesiastical seminary, where he seems to have principally devoted himself to the practice of athletic exercises. He came out in 1866 a clerk and a gymnasiarch rolled in one, and was appointed to the pastoral charge of Hernialde, a cluster of houses near Tolosa. He attended zealously to the duties of his ministry, leading a simple, frugal life with his sister; but when stories of the struggles of Zumalacárregui and Gonzales Moreno in the previous Carlist war were recounted by the wide hearth, it was noticed that the priest's eyes blazed like the faggots sputtering in flame-spikes towards the chimney-top. He was a Monarchist of the Basque stamp by race, by education, by conviction. He should have been a warrior, not a preacher of the Gospel; but if the circumstances which produce the man had not arisen, he might have vegetated and died in obscurity in his mountain village. The circumstances arose in August, 1870. A revolt of the four provinces of Alava, Guipúzcoa, and Biscay (the Basques or Vascongadas), and Navarre, was to take place in that month. At the outset it was rendered abortive by the treachery of a Colonel Escoda. It broke out on the 27th of August, and was suppressed on the following day. Santa Cruz, whose opinions were well known to the party, had been asked to watch over a depot of arms which had been collected for the insurgents at Hernialde. His share in the plot was betrayed, and one morning, as he was celebrating Divine Service, his church was entered by a party of soldiers who waited at the foot of the altar until he had finished the ceremony.

"In the name of the law, follow me," said the officer in command; "I have a warrant for your arrest from Madrid."

"Very well," said the Cura; "but surely you will allow me to breakfast first, unless they ordered you to take me captive on an empty stomach."

This was murmured in a tone so dulcet and injured that the officer hastened to assure the clergyman that he might breakfast, and accompanied him to the presbytery.

"Sin ceremonia," said the Cura, "will you condescend to share my meal?"

"Thanks, very much."

The priest entered the house; the soldiers waited outside, and argued that it was an infernal shame and a piece of tyranny on the part of Prim and the rest to have ordered such a harmless, nice man to be clapped into gaol. Presently a peasant with a basket of fruit on his head came out of the house. The soldiers waited long. They waited in vain. The peasant and the priest were one and the same.

For two years Santa Cruz wandered in the mountains and in France, was "on his keeping," as they say in Munster, but was finally arrested and interned at Nantes, by the French authorities. A characteristic story was related of his arrest. He was stopped on the bridge between St. Jean de Luz and Cibour by two gendarmes.

"Your papers?" demanded one.

"My papers! Wait till I look for them," answered Santa Cruz, not in the least disconcerted.

He fumbled in his pockets, turned them inside out, tapped the lining of his clothes, searched high and low, pretending to be very much astonished that he could not discover the document; and, suddenly, while the gendarmes, thrown off their guard, were speaking to one another, made a spring sideways, and was off like a bolt from a bow, the agents of authority pounding after him in their clumsy jack-boots. The chase lasted an hour, to the intense amusement of all the idlers of the town; but a peasant, not grasping the true state of affairs, clutched the panting Santa Cruz and held him until the arrival of the gendarmes.

In 1872, when Don Carlos again made appeal to arms, Santa Cruz succeeded in evading notice, and crossing the frontier, attached himself as chaplain to the band of Recondo. The Pretendiente himself entered by the pass of Vera, but was surprised at Oroquieta, in Navarre, by General Moriones, who defeated him on the 4th of May, and withered his hopes for that time. The convention of Amorovieta followed, arms were given up by thousands, and the factions, or partidas, dispersed to their homes. Santa Cruz returned to France. After a week's interval he re-entered Spain, and joined a body of the insurgents who still ranged the hills in Guipúzcoa. One day he missed his companions in a forced march, and fell into an ambuscade.

"I am Santa Cruz," he said to the soldiers, unquailingly, "do what you will with me."

He was pinioned and led to the nearest village.

The commandant of the detachment, one Urdanpilleta, went up to his prisoner and said to him, with an inexcusable pettiness of sarcasm:

"My good lad, you are out of luck. In a few hours you are safe to be shot."

"All right. We shall see about that," stoically answered Santa Cruz.

The priest was led into a large two-storied house, and thrust into a room near the garret, there to enter on his preparation for death. There was a bed in the room, and from the sheets on that bed Santa Cruz made the rosary on which to tell his litany, which was not one for the dying. He tore them up, twisted them, tied them together, and letting himself out of the window as far as his improvised rope would go, dropped into the arms of a couple of friends beneath. Before the alarm could be given he was up to his neck in a marsh, where his head was concealed by a rank growth of rushes. After an enforced bath of twelve hours he sought refuge with a wood-cutter, who helped him to pass over by night into France. The tale of his escape added to his fame. He was no longer a cura, he was a cabecilla—a born leader in partisan warfare. The Carlists still kept the field in Catalonia, but in the north-west all was apparently over. Order reigned as in Warsaw. Nevertheless, it was felt that a spark would rekindle a conflagration. Santa Cruz was the spark.

"If I had only thirty men at my back, I'd lift the flag again," Santa Cruz was overheard to boast.

The thirty men presented themselves; and, on the 1st of December, 1872, the irrepressible priest, now surnamed the Peter the Hermit of Carlism, recrossed the frontier. Six days afterwards he stopped the mail train a few miles outside San Sebastian, and Madrid learned with stupor that the Carlist insurrection had flared up anew.

"That was virtually the knell of the Savoy dynasty," said my informant, "and Santa Cruz it was who tolled the knell."

This notable individuality must have the rare magnetic power of compelling men to follow and believe in him, and of winning over their fidelity. His band of thirty has now swelled to five hundred, as devoted as ever were the Highlanders of Preston and Falkirk. He believes in his star; and he does not believe in carrying on hostilities with kid-gloves on his hands. Vitriol is more in his line than rose-water. I should very much like to meet Santa Cruz. He is said to be as agile as Mina, a wonderful walker, and to share all the fatigues and privations of his followers. He accomplished an almost incredible journey across the craggy hills and ravines, from Tafalla in Navarre to the confines of Biscay, in sixteen hours. At sunset, when the halt is called, and the provisions are distributed, the guerrilleros assemble round their chief, who resumes for a time the character of the Cura of Hernialde. Evening devotions are repeated, and prayers are offered for his Majesty King Charles VII., the Much-Desired; for Spain and her rescue from the monster of anarchy; for the dead, and for those who are next to die on the "campo de honor." The devotions ended, the priest again becomes the partisan-chief, and praises or blames his soldiers; and then the guards are set, and the guerrilleros, wrapped in their blankets, take a final pull at the wine-skin, and sink to rest upon the heather. Long after the band has been shrouded in mist lethargic, the figure of Santa Cruz may be seen looming against a rock, upright but for the head, which is supported by a huge gnarled staff. In his hand he grasps a key. When the benumbed or listless fingers part and release that key four times, Santa Cruz gives the rousing signal, the guerrilleros start to their feet, and the line of march is again taken up.

Is it not all delightfully romantic? If the late Miss Jane Porter, who wrote that prized book of truant youth, "The Scottish Chiefs," were only to have encountered this pretty man, she would have swooned with the joy of authorship. Had Harrison Ainsworth but dreamed of such unconventional possibilities, he would never have debased his intellect to the glorification of a vulgar prison-breaker like Jack Sheppard. But the only craftsman of the pen who could have risen to the height of the theme was he who wove the gold-shot tale of "Paul Clifford."

The latest news we hear of the Carlist priest is that a woman was shot by his orders at Escoriaza.[A] On second thought I am not so sure that I should very much like to meet Santa Cruz. And at this very period, while the shrieks of a fusilladed female were ringing in the air, a fussy committee of dilettante Carlists, sitting in London, protested that the sacred cause of legitimacy was advancing by lawful, chivalric, and immaculate means only! From the snug security of their back-parlour they wrote letters to the papers denying the "wanton" destruction of railway-stations by the Carlists. The flames were still undulating over the station of Santa Olla, between Burgos and Pancorbo, while the ink was wet on that inspired refutation! There are factories of falsehood elsewhere than in Spain.

A cabecilla had warned the station-masters in Guipúzcoa that all railway-servants who durst perform their work would be shot, and that all trains which had the hardihood to move would be given over to the flames; and Lizárraga, an ex-field-officer of the regular army, had calmly notified to the alcaldes of the province that he would fine them what would be the equivalent of a hundred pounds sterling with us the first time they failed to advise him of the movements of troops, and that he would stick them up against a wall and put a bullet through their heads for the second offence. Passports through the Carlist lines, formally drawn up, sealed, and signed, were for sale for ten duros (about two pounds sterling) in bureaux transparently dissembled, and met with ready purchasers. The article was cheap, if only as a curiosity. Here is the textual copy of an announcement in La Esperanza, a recognised and tolerated Carlist organ of Madrid:

"The direction of the Northern Railway Company having failed to observe the neutrality ordered respecting the conveyance of troops and stores of war, the Carlists, we are assured, cut the line yesterday at four points in the province of Guipúzcoa."

The Republic that permitted a newspaper published under its nose thus to talk of rebels against its authority "ordering" the railway companies not to convey troops was not arbitrary, to my thinking. But Spain is an enigma. An English Government would hardly permit a journal to speak of the operations of a Fenian band in the same terms.

There could be no concealment of the fact that the adherents of Charles VII., king *in nubibus*, were making headway.

On the 9th of March a combat was fought at Monreal, a village on the slope of a hill to the south-east of Pampeluna, between the factions of Dorregaray, Ollo, Perula, and others, and the regulars under Nouvilas, the General who had set out from the capital with such a grandiloquent farewell speech. Pampeluna is distant sixteen hours by rail. The account of the combat, the most important since Oroquieta, was published in the official journal four days afterwards.

In the interval the Carlist papers at Madrid had been singing hosannas over an alleged victory of their friends, and boasting that the Republican General had lost his artillery. The Republican Government did not suppress those papers. As a matter of course, Nouvilas claimed the victory for himself. Victories are always claimed by both sides in this civil struggle. To get near truth one must read the narratives for and against, compare and balance them, and by jealous analysis of evidence it is possible one may light, in a haphazard way, on something vaguely resembling what actually happened.

The report of Nouvilas is before me as I write. He estimated the enemy at 2,500 infantry and 200 cavalry. His own force, consisting of a battalion of the Chasseurs of Porto Rico, two companies of the Guadalajara infantry, a section of mountain artillery (two guns, I take it), a couple of sections of the Hussars of Pavia, and one of the Lancers of Numancia, made up a total of about 600 foot and 80 horse. The combat lasted through two hours of darkness, and Nouvilas, although bragging that he dislodged the Carlists, has to admit that he was unable to follow up his success. Reason: his troops had marched eight leagues without food or rest! A league is 4,565 English yards; multiply that by eight, and I think it will be suspected that the tale of Nouvilas was intended for the amphibious branch of the service. He confesses to a loss of one superior officer (Colonel Don Manuel Ibarreta, of the Staff Corps), and five rank and file killed, three officers and fifty-three wounded, six *contused*, and four missing.

An anecdote casts a lurid light of disclosure on the discipline of this victorious column. The Staff Corps have a museum at Madrid, and were anxious to procure some relics of their comrade who had "died gloriously while holding a hazardous position with singular courage." All they could get was his cap and sash. His boots were pulled off, his pockets rifled, and every little article he possessed, to his English lever watch, was appropriated— doubtless by soldiers who were desirous of souvenirs of so gallant a gentleman.

Certain inferences were to be drawn from the report of Nouvilas. The Carlist position was admirably chosen, the leaders took proper precautions against surprise, and the men fought with dogged pluck. They must have been badly equipped, since they left behind them firearms of every description. They are armed anyhow; some carry fowling-pieces, some blunderbusses, and some fight with sticks and stones, as the return of those six soldiers contused establishes. The General had breechloaders and mountain howitzers; hussars and cuirassiers supported his infantry; and yet these rebels of the hills held their own for two hours!

Even on his own showing the victory of the Republican commander was poor, and dearly purchased. At one time he admits he was encircled by the enemy, and had to unsheath in self-defence. He reports four men missing— that means captured; and, though having routed his foes, he can only point to thirteen prisoners and two dead horses! The Carlists fled "precipitately," but they appear to have had leisure to carry off their wounded with the exception of sixteen. Reference to Carlists supposed to be wounded, coupled with the silence about those supposed to be dead, is remarkable. Were there none killed? General Nouvilas, instead of going forward next day, returned to Pampeluna to indite a despatch in which he directly commends his own four sons, and indirectly praises himself. He has been laid up with sore throat since, and has been unable to resume his prosecution of the dislodged and dispersed enemy. I begin to think these Carlists, as my landlord at Beasain predicted, "will give more trouble."

CHAPTER X.

Barbarism of Tauromachy—A Surreptitious Ticket—The Novillos—Islington *not* Madrid—Apology for Cock-Fighting—Maudlin Humanity—The Espada a Popular Idol—In the Bull-Ring—A Precious "Ster-oh"—The Trumpets Speak—The Procession—Play of the Quadrille—The Defiance—"Bravo, Cucharra!"—"Bravo, Toro!" The Blemish of the Sport—An Indignant English Lassie.

CONSTANTINE, the porter at the Fonda de Paris, asked me one forenoon would I like to take a ticket for a bull-fight. He had an excellent one (excellent batch, he meant) to dispose of "in the shade." I stared at him indignantly, nodded my head in the same vein, but winked as I passed through the hall and sprang up the stairs. An English clergyman and his daughter, who had expressed an abhorrence for tauromachy in my presence, had overheard Constantino's temptation, and hence my behaviour.

"Tauromachy!" the dear old minister argued. "What can you expect, sir, from a people who have to buckle two languages in double harness to find a name for their brutal practice? 'Tis illegitimate, sir, like the derivative. *Taurus* is Latin, μάχη is Greek; the compound is barbaric."

I bowed, for Emmeline was seemly, with a delicate elegance, and she looked up with a pleased and almost triumphant look, as much as to say, Papa is not one of your common persons, but a mighty learned dignitary indeed.

That was why Constantine waited his opportunity to slip the ticket into my hands in a corridor, explaining that a seat in the shade was a privilege not to be despised, as the sun at the other side flung a glare on the spectator that dazzled his view; besides, it was broiling and headachy to sit for hours in its rays.

"I knew you would go the first chance you had," said Constantine; "I read it in your eyes as you gloated over the pictures of the sport in the hall. They make a magnificent fan, or you could hang them up on the wall in your house in England; I can let you have a lot a bargain. I was sure of it when you stopped opposite the placard of the corrida outside, and shook yourself with joy."

Constantine was a good judge of human nature. I would as soon think of visiting Madrid and not seeing a bull-fight, as of visiting Constantinople and not hunting after the dancing dervishes; Kandy, and not gazing on the Perra Harra procession; London in the season, and not going to the Military Tournament.

But, as I afterwards learned, the weather was still too cold for the genuine game; this might be regarded as a rehearsal, but was patronized by the connoisseurs, as there were openings for criticism on the style of novices, and estimates as to who had in them the stuff of coming men. The bull wants the ardent heats of midsummer to fire him for the combat. The true season begins with a late Easter-tide, when the kings of the herd, fresh from the meadows, have arrogant blood careering in their veins, and are supple in the limbs. To stimulate them now, the dogs or the banderillas de fuego, both alien to true tauromachy, would have to be called in. This is but the heyday of the novillos, the unripe beasts, with india-rubber or wooden balls blunting their half-developed horns, who are sent into the arena to be at the mercy of youths ambitious to become chulos. The novillos prance and frisk and toss their adversaries; it is a frolic and no more. Months afterwards I saw a band of blind mendicants armed with long sticks descend into the ring at Murcia, and succeed, some of them, in keeping off the novillos. As well as giving youngsters the favour of familiarizing themselves with the capa, used to irritate the bull, this practice puts the animal himself into good wind, and teaches him what he has to expect when he is admitted into the pit of the amphitheatre for the final tussle. Your common bull is not apt for these duels; he must be a bull of race, haughty and high-spirited, before he is welcomed as a gladiator *moriturus*. There are stock-breeders in Castile and Andalusia renowned for the superb stamp of their cattle; and of these, not the least renowned is a noble count who bears the name and is a descendant of Christopher Columbus. But the immature tomfoolery has no more resemblance to the stern, actual diversion than a donkey-race has to the Derby. The description in "Childe Harold" is spirited, but has been pared down to accommodate itself to the exigencies of rhyme. Byron when he wrote it must have had a spasm of squeamishness. But that must have been a gorgeous function at the marriage of Isabella, when a public square was converted into an amphitheatre, Toro was monarch for days consecutive, and the bonniest cavaliers of Spain, clad in jackets glimmering with gems, entered the lists against him.

In England, where patronizing leading-articles are indited about those semi-civilized Spaniards, whenever a toreador is injured in the exercise of his profession, nothing would seem to be really known about the sport, and yet there is a self-sufficient assumption among persons called "well-informed" that they know all about it. Speaking once with a colleague of the press at Madrid, the representative of a very great English paper, I was told almost the only instructions he had received on leaving London were not to write anything of bull-fighting, or "hackneyed rubbish of that sort." Yet no nearer approach to bull-fighting has ever been witnessed in England than a silly simulacrum at the Agricultural Hall. The first calf that was enlarged from the make-believe toril on that occasion quietly proceeded to nibble a scrap of paper on the tan. The toreadores were real toreadores, but the bulls were not of the fiery breed of Andalusia. If they had been, the agents of the Society for the Prevention of Cruelty to Animals would have thought twice before venturing into the same enclosure with them to bar the entertainment on the score of cruelty. Still, the enterprising public caterer who had brought over the quadrille of bull-fighters was wise in his generation. Had the legitimate article been given, there was enough foretokening of patronage on the opening night to prove it would have been a great success.

I call bull-fighting a glorious pastime. In my mental vision I can mark the rising gorge of some splenetic Briton of the philanthropic school as he reads this phrase, "glorious pastime," wipes his glasses and reads it again. How am I wrong? It is savage, bloodthirsty, and debasing, he will say. Therein I join issue with him, though I may bring a censorious pile of cant crumbling and clattering about my ears. Cock-fighting was once popular in these islands, and that not so long ago. I have often played truant from school, and challenged a thrashing, to drain the high pleasures of a well-contested main. The late Admiral Rous and the late Lord Derby were admirers of the sport, and if I am not mistaken the rules governing a London pit sometimes patronized by royalty had a place in the earlier editions of Hoyle. The best apology for cock-fighting I ever heard was made by an eccentric uncle of mine, who asked his censor, "Why did God put the fighting drop into the game-cock's veins but that he might fight when he got the chance?"

There is cruelty, peradventure, in attaching long steel spurs, keen as bradawls, to the cocks' legs, as there is in supplying men-at-arms with swords and rifles instead of letting them wage war against one another with teeth and feet and fists—the weapons of nature. Chanticleer of the martial breed should be put into the ring with his natural spurs.

Well, in Spain he is, for the sport flourishes there still; and one of my recollections of my last day in Madrid is having sacrificed a meal to be present at the Circo de Gallos, the recognised building where combats of the kind are carried on in a well-filled amphitheatre, with roped platform in the centre, and seats in tiers around. The roadway in front was lined with equipages, and the curled darlings of the Madrilene aristocracy stepped in to witness the tournament and bet on the result; but I own the gentler sex I never met there. There are rules to regulate the conduct of the matches posted conspicuously on the walls; there are scales to weigh the combatants, lemons to clean their spurs, a regular staff of heelers, time-keepers, and umpires; the fixtures are given in the newspapers in the same column as the theatrical programme, and the guardians of public order are always in attendance. On the same principle bull-fighting is conducted, and the same argument holds good in favour of its retention.

This babble of cruelty is veriest wind-bag humanity, and, logically, has not a leg to stand upon. To confront the king of the herd in the arena is bolder and braver than to course the hare at Altcar, or shoot pigeons at Hurlingham, or make a battue of pheasants in a Norfolk preserve—sports to which our patricians are disposed, sports which are chronicled in the fashionable organs with apparent approval. There is more risk to those who share in a bull-fight than in knocking ponies about on the polo-ground at Preston, sawing their mouths and breaking their shins, or in worrying the fox over the pastures of Leicestershire. As for that cold-blooded, cowardly, treacherous recreation of the contemplative man, flinging bait to a harmless defenceless fish, and luring him to a painful end, it is a piece of deliberate barbarism not to be mentioned in the same breath with bull-fighting. And yet Mr. John Bright, who has the reputation of being a gentleman of chivalrous temper and pacific instincts, is said to be passionately fond of this recreation. Observe to what the reasoning of those who frantically protest against the national pastime of Spain reduces itself. So far, I wish it to be understood that I am arguing with the intent of establishing a *reductio ad absurdum*. If coursing, hunting, shooting, and fishing are justifiable—and I hold that they are—then on the like grounds are cock-fighting and bull-fighting justifiable. The beasts on the earth, the birds of the air, and the fishes in the sea, are all created for man's use and benefit. To kill them is no crime, if the killing be not attended with the infliction of wanton pain. The destiny of the minor order of creation is to minister to the appetites or necessities of the lord of creation; and pleasurable excitement is a necessity. The objections to the position here taken up are untenable, except by maudlin and maundering humanitarians, who think more of the life of a pet poodle than of the life of their fellow-man, and by that lost section of mild lunatics, the vegetarians.

Having said so much in defence of bull-fighting, I may be permitted, in entering into details of the diversion, to anticipate experiences and knowledge which did not come to me until later on. The further my acquaintance with the ring extended, the more convinced I became that tauromachy will last as long as Spain lasts. It has blemishes, like other recreations. To my thinking, the chief is that Toro goes into the sanded arena foredoomed to die. No matter how pluckily he fights, no matter what play he shows, the cachetero awaits him. Then there is torture, but an unavoidable torture, in the mode in which horses are killed. I well remember what an acclimatized aficionado, M. de Coutuly, of the Paris *Temps*, said to me in a discussion on the point:

"These horses are under capital sentence when they are helped to the grace of a historic death in the amphitheatre; they are rescued *en route* to the knacker's-yard; but, bah! it is useless to try to convince men with English prejudices. With you, the horse is more valuable than the man."

Thorough garrons these horses are in old Spain; but in the South American countries, colonized from Spain, I am told they bring spirited barbs into the ring, who can bite and kick, and take their own part generally, and who sometimes clear the bull at a bound, as he advances to the attack.

If tauromachy will last in Spain as long as Spain lasts, so likewise will those who practise the art he held in honour. No names are guarded in fonder reverence there to-day than those of Montes, Pepete, and Pepe-Hillo; and when Frascuelo was wounded, his residence was besieged by sympathizing inquirers. The bulletins of his health were read as anxiously as if they were issued from a royal palace. Bouquets, pastry, and billets-doux were laid in tribute on the mat of his bedchamber, and the sweetest and proudest dames of the sweet and proud patrician houses of Castile—houses with sangre azul unsuspicious in their veins, and thirteen grandees in their pedigree—sent to inquire after the condition of the famous espada. Tom Sayers was never more idolized in England than Frascuelo is in Spain. And so, in like manner, are his compeers, Lagartijo, and the rest. This liking for them is pushed to excess, much as the cult for heroes of the prize-ring was with us in a past generation. Once I was roused from a nap by Liberato, a faithful body-man, shuffling his feet to the sprightly movements of a bolero. His eyes twinkled like laughing fire, his gitano-tinted cheeks had a tawny-purple grape-flush. He was under a high-pressure of exhilaration, and instinctively sought to relieve himself by dancing.

"Liberato?"

"Caballero."

"What devil possesses thee? Hast got a tress of thy ama's hair, or fallen upon a treasure-box of Boabdil?"

"Señor, I am proud as a hidalgo this day. You know Frascuelo?"

"Si, si."

"I have seen him; I have heard him speak."

"Dios mio! If it be not a poor jest on thy part, thou'rt a happy man."

"No jest, señor; and hearken!" approaching and lowering his voice: "he sat at the same table with me, and," this impressively and confidentially, "he shook hands with me as we parted!"

"Caramba! Let me shake that hand."

Laugh at this anecdote, but did not a New York hack-driver make a small fortune by letting out for osculatory purposes the hand that helped Jenny Lind from her carriage? Have not strawberries touched by the lips of Lydia Thompson fetched a guinea each at a dramatic *fête*, and photographs of Sara

Bernhardt, signed with her sign-manual, run up to an alarming figure at the Albert Hall? Have I not myself been privy to the offer by a British matron of sums incredible for the straw through which the Prince of Wales had sucked a sherry-cobbler at the Paris Exhibition of 1867?

"Ster-oh!" ejaculated the negro waiter with open mouth. "Why, bress you, dat's no use, we trowed it away; but, as yer a nice ole lady, heah's a dozen for nuffin!"

The spectacle in the Plaza de Toros, the spacious unroofed area surrounded by stone benches rising one above another, away to the sheltered balconies up high at the back, is one of the most enlivening that imagination can conceive on the afternoon of a corrida, when male and female humanity, all jubilant bustle and expectancy, make a prismatic girdle around. Fans move with an incessant tremulous flutter; there is a continuous susurrus of voices, broken by occasional hoarse bursts of laughter at some mishap, or hoarse roars of welcome as some favourite enters; the regal sun discharges his fierce messages of light from his throne of blue, and the costumes of every colour, wavering with the pulsations of the throng, are an active kaleidoscope, most vivid and variegated. We are in our places. We have stepped up the Alcalá at the heels of the picquet of armed militia charged with the maintenance of order. We have threaded our way through the rough maze of passages to our palco, peeping at the stable where the sorry horses are kept, at the room where the toreadores dress themselves, and at the little oratory where the matador prays before he stalks into the palestra. We are in our places, and everybody is in his place; the Governor of the city in his box of state yonder. While the music races over the assemblage in glad alternation of rush and ripple, let us look below. There is a strong wooden barrier some six feet high around the arena, and at knee-height, on the inner side of this barrier, there is a berme to help the pursued chulo to a footing as he vaults over into the surrounding lane formed by this interior and an exterior barrier. This lane is guarded by policemen, and is so narrow that a bull has not room to turn in it; for bulls sometimes bound over the inner barrier. When that occurs, and I have seen it occur not seldom, they are driven round until they reach one of the gates opening into the ring. The trumpets and tymbals speak warning; a profound silence falls upon the crowd for an instant, and then from a side passage enters the cavalcade we have awaited—enters to a stately martial march. First, the mounted alguazil in his ancient garb, plumed, cloaked, funereal; then the chulos, lithe, young, graceful; then the picadores on their garrons, Mexican-looking in their saddles, with tall pummel and crupper and shovel-shaped stirrups, wide-leafed sombreros, their short jackets tagged all over, their yellow breeches and their high boots lead-lined; then the banderilleros, and then the matador, the chieftain of the troop. The alguazil beseeches the key of the toril from the Governor, receives it, turns it in the lock; and as the bull with dazed vision enters into the sunshine at one gate, he disappears at an amble through another.

The bull! What a noble specimen of his race!—broad-browed, clean-horned, and clean-limbed; high courage in his bloodshot orbs, his dilated nostril, and his lashing tail! On the right and left the quadrille arrange themselves, the picadores, each with a spike at the end of his long shaft, and a kerchief bandaging one eye of his horse; the chulos, pretty fellows in turban, loose embroidered jackets, ruffled shirts, kneebreeches of coquettish hue and texture, silken hose and buckled shoes, standing, with their cloaks, nearer to the centre of the ring. All these toreadores are men of symmetry and power, all wear chignons in nets, and are close-shaven, except as to side-whiskers of the brief "mutton-chop" order, and all bear themselves as if they were proud of their vocation. The bull waits. The chulos give challenge. They rush upon him, shaking their gaudy little cloaks, and as he charges they scamper to the sides, while one takes up the running from another. In short, they tease him as much for the sake of tiring him out as of testing his disposition. But by-and-by one chulo ingeniously leads the charging bull towards a horse. Toro rushes head-foremost. The picador is unequal to keep him off with his spike; the horse is gored in the belly and overthrown, the rider falling under. The chulos cluster to the rescue, with their fluttering cloaks, and draw the bull away confused. The picador is extricated; the horse is taken out, and in a few moments after re-enters, his entrails packed inside and stomach sewn up, and is once more offered to the maddened brute, always on his blind side. We shall hurry over this episode of the tournament; I do not like it, nor do you. But here is something really fine. The banderilleros enter, with barbed shafts decked with ribbons, poised in each hand, and make a feinting advance on the bull, and as he runs to meet them they deftly hurl their shafts and elude him by a demi-volte. The act of doing this well is to plant one banderilla on each side of the bull's neck, close by the streaming favours that mark the herd from which he is furnished—the colours of his stable, so to speak—to plant them evenly and at equal distances from his crest, and when this is skilfully accomplished there are frantic yells of praise, and caps and cigars are showered into the arena. When the banderillero is awkward, they rain on him with potatoes. These banderilleros incur hazard. I have seen one so keenly chased by the bull that he was pinned against the barriers by the bull's horns as he was in the act of vaulting over. Pinned, but not in the flesh; the branching horns stuck in the wood at either side, just above the calf of one leg, and imprisoned him until he had to be sawed out.

This is but the prologue; now for the play. Toro by this time is in a white rage; there is foam at his chaps, his steaming sides are laced with blood. Cucharra of Puerto Santa Maria is the matador. Majestically he strides towards the Governor's box, stoops in obeisance, and in a loud voice makes proclamation: "Brindo por Puerto Santa Maria, por toda su compañia, por el vulgo de Madrid; voy á matar ese bicho ó el bicho me mata á mi;" an address which may thus be freely rendered: "I pledge myself to Puerto Santa Maria and all its society, and to the people of Madrid; and now I am ready to kill this animal, if the animal cannot kill me." He removes his turban, and, with a graceful jerk with his right hand from behind his back over his left shoulder, flings it into the Governor's box, as a gage of his boasted prowess. He takes his straight keen-tempered sword and his cloak of offensive scarlet, and advances towards the bull. Now is the supreme trial, now is the time when men let their lighted cigarettes drop from their mouths and clench their teeth; now is the time when women close their fans and draw long breaths. Cucharra faces Toro at a yard's distance. They regard each other. Cucharra hides his sword under his cloak, and presents it to the bull. Toro lowers his head, shuts his eyes, and charges, but the toreador gracefully slips aside and saves his life by a turn of the heel. Three times he repeats the feat of this risksome pirouette; but woe to him if he is an instant too late in his movements, or if the soil is treacherous. The fourth time, as the bull lowers his head, Cucharra lifts himself on his toes, and with one sure swift blow plunges the blade, almost to the hilt, into the spine of his antagonist. The bull stands; there is a shout of "Bravo!" the bull still stands, ten seconds, twenty, thirty; there is a howl of disappointment; but Cucharra gazes contemptuously around; he knows he has done his work well, and, my faith, he has. Toro quivers and drops, and Cucharra plants a foot on the neck of his prostrate enemy. The bull has died of internal hæmorrhage; not a drop of blood has distilled from his mouth. Bravo, Cucharra!

This death at the first thrust—death without drip of the crimson fluid from the mouth—is the artistic death. When the sword pierces at the wrong spot, is displaced by the shaking of the bull, and sent flying, gore-wet, through the air, it is awkward workmanship.

But Toro showed "mucho fuego" before he was so neatly pierced in the medulla. Bravo, Toro! And now the cachetero stoops over him, and, with one dig of his sharp knife in the neck, makes assurance doubly sure. The team of mules trot in, and trot out again with the dead champion at their heels; and the urchins outside are dancing on his carcase as the drums and tymbals give prelude to the entrance of a second champion into the enthusiastic circle.

The slimy pools in the arena are promptly strewn with sand, and the fresh bull is ushered into the lists, either against the same quadrille, or against another espada with his special troop of assistants. Some of the brutes are self-possessed, as that "proud and stately steer" Harpado of Xarama, who was matched with Ganzul the Moor.

"Dark is his hide on either side, but the blood within doth boil,

And the dun hide glows, as if on fire, as he paws to the turmoil,

His eyes are jet, and they are set in crystal rings of snow;

But now they stare with one red glare of brass upon the foe."

All in vain, Toro. Thy fate is sealed. Useless to prance round with defiance, to bellow with unsatisfied wrath, to churn the sand with furious hoof and flash hither and thither the flaming arrows of thy glance. Thou art foredoomed, and wilt fall as surely after brave struggle as thy mate, less eager for the strife, who has to be pricked up to anger, and drops at last bewildered amid the derision of the crowd. That is where I find fault with the sport. Toro who shows good fight should get his respite, like the Roman gladiator who pleased the multitude.

Still, is his fate to be deplored? Confess, is it not rather to be envied? He gives up his vital principle in the rapture of battle; he feels no wound but the grievous one to the combatant that he can beat down no more foes; he yields breath with a bold front; there is threat in his agony as he sinks, still with challenge in his port, amid the applause of admiring thousands. There is something of martyr-heroism in this ending. It is grander, nobler, happier than to fall by the butcher's plebeian mallet in the slaughter-house, or to succumb to the slow miseries of rinderpest. Whoso denies it will downface me next that it is fitter for the warrior to die of podagra in a four-post bed than to perish on the field with harness on his back—that dropsy at St. Helena was more to be coveted than a bullet at Waterloo!

Tauromachy, I repeat, will last as long as Spain lasts. It will have its school and its dialect, its canons of skill expatiated upon in elaborate treatises; its honoured exponents; its impassioned amateurs and its munificent patrons; its historiographers and poets. In my devotedness to it I have sacrificed the favour of a comely English maiden, for Emmeline, who has seen through my hypocrisy in the hall, averts the light of her countenance as we sit down to dinner. I am sorry for it, for I had inclinings towards that lady, she was so attentive to her father, and she had confided to me with such a pretty frankness that she sighed for the days when Mohammad-al-Hamar was throned in Granada.

NOTE BY THE WRITER'S DAUGHTER.—The conceit of you. Emmeline, I think, was quite right to cut you, after your brutishness. No doubt you think the glorification of bull-butchery a piece of fine writing, and so original, you know. I'm up to the games of you authors; but if I were the printers I would not print one single line of it. I should just like to put a pen in the bull's hand and read *his* description of the fight.

CHAPTER XI.

The Shamrock of Erin and Olive of Spain—Hispano-Hibernian Regiments—The Spanish Soldier—An Unpopular Hidalgo—Flaw in the Harness—The Organization of the Army—The Guardia Civil—The Cavalry, Engineers, and Infantry—General Cordova—The Disorganization of the Army—Mutiny in Pampeluna—Officers Out of Work—Turbulent Barcelona—Irresolute Contreras—Pistolet Discharges Himself—The Madrid Garrison.

IN Moore's "Melodies" crops up a martial lyric, in which there is a jingling reference at the end of every verse to the shamrock of Erin and olive of Spain. Here is about the pith of its sentiment:

"May his tomb want a tear and a name,

Who would ask for a nobler, a holier death,

Than to turn his last sigh into victory's breath,

For the Shamrock of Erin and Olive of Spain!"

The Blakes and O'Donnells are apostrophized; but as well as I can make out what the bard is driving at, he had Wellington and his companions in his mind's eye.

There had been closer and earlier and longer ties than those of the campaigns against the French between Spain and Ireland. According to the annals of the Four Masters (translated by the father of the late Edmond O'Donovan), the Clanna-Milidh set sail from Galicia and invaded the Emerald Isle in the year 1698 before the Christian era. They established the Milesian dynasty, which lasted two thousand eight hundred and seventy years—rather a better record than we meet in Bulgaria, modern Greece, and sometimes even in Spain itself. Galway, *teste* Kohl, carries the imagination to Granada and Valencia. At the beginning of the eighteenth century there were six Irish regiments at least in the Spanish service, namely, those of Hibernia, Irlanda, Limerick, Ultonia, and Waterford (all infantry), and the Dragoons of Dublin. There was also an infantry regiment called Conacia, or Wauchop, after its commander, one of a fighting family well known in the Lothians. There were officers of my name in the Limerick and Ultonia corps, as there are in the Spanish army still.[B] Most of these Irish organizations were disbanded at the close of the last century, and all had lost their purely Irish character, although the titles, Hibernia, Ultonia, and Irlanda, were retained on the list till 1833.

Naturally, and because of profession and certain associations, I took an interest in soldiers, and, at the risk of offending the lady-reader who is waiting for the romantic part of this book, I intend to devote a chapter to the Spanish army. Such judgment as I have to offer is formed not alone upon what I saw at Madrid, but afterwards, when I had opportunity of watching the troops at work. Before going any further, I may unreservedly confess that I hold a high opinion of the Spanish soldier. He is sober, enduring, brave, and an indefatigable marcher. Better raw material for warfare, I am sure, could not readily be come at, and I am equally sure that if more attention were paid to drill, and if the curse of morbid aspirations for promotion amongst the lower grades were more rigidly repressed, the Spanish army would regain its ancient renown. This restless and diseased ambition is not to be traced to the rank and file, but to those immediately above them, the men with a puffed-up idea of themselves, and a smattering of education, and is often developed by the connivance of their immediate superiors. Let us take an example. In 1866 there was an uprising in favour of Prim, headed by the sergeants of artillery at the San Gil barracks, in Madrid. Captain Hidalgo was privy to the plot, which eventuated in a fiasco, but not before sundry officers of the regiment had lost their lives. A large number of the sergeants were summarily shot a few days afterwards. Hidalgo escaped. In the November of 1872, Hidalgo, then a General, was appointed Master-General of the Ordnance by Amadeus. Amongst the artillery there is a strong *esprit de corps*, and the officers in a body declared they would resign unless the appointment were cancelled. They did not object to Hidalgo on account of his implication in mutiny, which is a recognised institution in the Spanish army, but because they believed he had previous knowledge that some of his brother-officers would be sacrificed, and never gave them a word of warning or raised a plea in their behalf. The want of comradeship was his crime, and the resignations of those who protested against it were accepted in a bulk.

At the time I was in Madrid the artillery was in a state of demoralisation. The captains of the scientific force were all promoted sergeants, and the old officers were idly parading the streets in plain clothes. Amadeus had certainly committed a foolish act, although he may have justified himself to himself by the reflection that in approving an appointment made by his Ministers he was behaving loyally, and that by a wholesale rejection of the demand of the discontented officers he would set up an iron precedent against insubordination. He never paused to think that he was stripping Spain of a vital portion of its harness. A sergeant may be an excellent practical gunner, and be able to lay a piece accurately; but that does not qualify him to command a battery. Scientific acquirements and training are necessary, a mastery of technique and tactics, quickness of resource, and the habit of authority. The promoted sergeants were wanting in these essentials, and the Carlists soon found out the weak spot in the armour.

The strength of the permanent army is fixed annually by the Cortes, and every Spaniard above the age of twenty is liable to be drawn, and has to serve four years under the flag. The nation is divided for military purposes into five captain-generalcies, the commandant of each of which holds a rank corresponding to a British field-marshal. The nominal strength of the infantry in round numbers is about 60,000; artillery, 9,500; engineers, 2,300; and cavalry, 11,500. Then there are the provincial militia, some 44,000 strong; the carabineros, or revenue police, 12,000; and the Guardia Civil, 10,000. These Civil Guards are picked men, robust, strapping, seasoned fellows, and are distributed over the country like the French gendarmery, to whose duties theirs are similar. They form a *corps d'élite*, and are the very mainstay of order. In fact, without them life and property during times of political commotion would very often be at the mercy of any horde of ragamuffins with weapons in their hands and the courage to use them. They are handsomely uniformed, wearing cocked-hats of the pattern of those to be seen in the prints of the First Napoleon, fine cloth tunics of dark blue, with epaulettes of white cord, and yellow side and cross-belts, and present a manful, soldierly appearance. From their valour and topographical knowledge they have been very serviceable in carrying on the guerrilla warfare with the Carlists, and are the terror of brigands and evil-doers. If all the troops were as orderly and well disciplined as these, Government would be easy, and those at its head might afford to be firm, regardless of mob clamour. In short, these magnificent Civil Guards are the best military force the country possesses. Some of them are mounted (and capitally mounted too), and all have an elevated notion of duty. A mutiny is never inaugurated by the Civil Guards. They stick to each other like wax, and are faithful to the powers that be, regardless of their political colour, so long as those powers are accepted by the nation. Dynasties may change and depart, as Ministries do; but the Guardia Civil is an organization immutable and goes on for ever. The one charge made against them has its warrant in necessity. When a prisoner is sent to gaol in some remote town under escort of the Civil Guards, he often makes an attempt to run away, and is invariably shot between the shoulders. No strict inquiry into the circumstances is made—it is an understood practice—a rascal is got rid of, to the relief of the community, by a quick and economic method, which is a desirable improvement on the laggard processes of law.

The cavalry is controlled by a director-general, who has a respectable staff of subordinates at his disposal. There are only two regiments of cuirassiers— the 1st, or King's; and the 2nd, or Queen's. There are two regiments of carabineers known as Calatrava and Bailen. There are eight regiments of lancers, viz., Farnesio, Villaviciosa, España, Sagunto, Santiago, Montesa, Numancia, and Lusitania. The hussar regiments are but two, Pavia and the Princess's. Prim's son, a boy of fifteen, was captain in the former, and the veteran Espartero honorary colonel of the latter. The name of a former colonel, Don Pedro Elio, "who died gloriously on the field of honour," like Latour d'Auvergne, first grenadier of France, is also borne on the rolls of the Princess's. There are six regiments of mounted chasseurs—namely, Almansa, Alcántara, Talavera, Albuera, Tetuan, and Castillejos, and two squadrons of Galicia and Mallorca respectively. These men, as far as I have seen, are well horsed, Andalusia furnishing some capital chargers, well-made and well-paced, and up to decent weights. There is nothing peculiar in the cavalry uniform, which is formed upon the French model. In fact, it would be difficult to distinguish the dragoons from the French dragoons, but that they have a seat and know how to keep it, and that their helmets are of a round Roman style, with a rising sun in a circuit of rays right in front.

The remount depôts are at Granada and Córdoba, and there are four establishments where sires for cavalry purposes are maintained at the expense of the State—namely, Córdoba, Baeza, Llerena, and Alcalá de Henares (the latter exclusively for the use of the mounted artillery). There is also a military school for the cavalry, maintained on the same system as that of the French at Saumur.

The Engineers are quite as tall but not so sturdy as our Grenadiers, and look up to their work. This was the favourite force of Prim, and it is only second to the Guardia Civil in its obedience to constituted authorities. From what I hear the men are carefully trained in sapping and mining, though of them, as of Spanish soldiers universally, one is compelled to say that they have too much leisure, and when soldiers have too much leisure the Devil invariably finds them occupation. The value of the artillery, which had been one of the best organizations of its class in Europe, as I have already said, at that precise epoch ranked at *nil*. Reports were circulated every day that the difficulties in this branch of the service had been arranged, but the wheels want such a dose of oil in Spain that one can never be certain that the machine is in order till it moves. The artillery is denuded of officers, and the infantry and cavalry have officers too often that are valueless; and in that lies the secret of the deterioration of an army which was once, and still might be made, capable of great things.

There are forty regiments of infantry, numbered as ours were, but known also by distinctive names, generally those of the locality in which each was originally raised. Thus the 1st Regiment is Rey, or the King's; the 2nd, Reina, or the Queen's; the 3rd, the Prince's; the 4th, the Princess's; the 5th, the Infante's; the 6th, the Regiment of Saboya; the 7th, of Africa; and then come those with territorial titles—the Regiments of Zamora, Soria, Córdoba, San Fernando, and so on, until we reach the 40th, which is called the Regiment of Málaga. The 14th, 29th, and 30th are respectively known as the Regiments of America, of the Constitucion, and of Iberia.

Each regiment consists of three battalions, except the 20th (the Guadalajara) and the 34th (the Granada), which have but two; and in each battalion there are six companies. Nominally, each company numbers about 80 rank and file, but he would be a wise man who could say how many answer to the roll-call in the existing state of disorganization. There are twenty-four battalions of handy light troops, who are equal to almost anything human in the way of marching. Agile and untiring, sound in wind and limb, they can get over an extraordinary length of ground with a speed that would not discredit professional walkers in England. The French foot-chasseur, who can put on an astonishing spurt now and again, is no rival to the Spanish cazador.

The infantry uniform is almost exactly that of the French—long grey capote, blue tunic with the number of the regiment on the collar, and red trousers. Instead of a shako the head is protected by a projecting cap of cloth and glaze, something like a stiffened Glengarry without ribbons. Those absurd white gaiters which gather dirt so quickly when it is wet under foot, and give the French soldier incessant bother to look after their pipe-claying, are replaced in the Spanish service by calfskin buskins and black cloth spatterdashes. Few more sensible uniforms are to be met with in Europe. Properly officered, there is nothing to prevent the Spanish infantry from regaining the prestige it once held. The men have the right stuff in them, are temperate and frugal, cheerful under privation, and hardy as wild ducks. They do not want pluck either; they have the reputation of showing a good deal of dash in their pursuit of the Carlists; but that is no fair criterion of what they could do when pitted against the troops of some great Power in ordered line of battle. Good lungs are indispensable in Carlist warfare, as an officer who was hunting them for six weeks in Catalonia, and never caught one, begged me to recollect. "You want men who can breast hills," he said. But good lungs are valuable in a campaign anywhere, and looking at these lively, well-set Spaniards as they trot along under their packs, I must say they favourably compare with those weakly men of the French line I saw staggering to the Eastern Railway Terminus at Paris, on their way to Metz, in 1870, or with some of the lank striplings I saw defiling before Victor Emmanuel at Somma in the autumn of 1872.

The Minister of War (Cordova) and the Minister of Marine (Béranger) are good. The general and the admiral had really no politics; but they knew their respective departments better than any men in Spain. Cordova comes of a fighting family, and "ran the army," to use an expressive Americanism, under Isabella, under the Serrano-Prim Administration, under Amadeus, and would, I dare say, under Don Carlos, if he came to-morrow. In fact, the general is a military Vicar of Bray, but for the less egotistical motive that he loves his profession, and does not care to see it and Spain go to the bad, which Spain would if the army did. But he is not a Republican, neither is

Béranger; and the sovereign people will only be governed by Republicans. They will not permit men of another party even to do them a service. Therefore the general and the admiral, and their colleagues of the Finance, Public Works, and the Colonies, have patriotically made up their minds to retire. Thus, for the moment, stands Spain, ruled by an Assembly divided against itself and an Executive in a state of dissolution.

Meanwhile the army is hurrying to the devil at the double-quick. The troops which fell back on Pampeluna, after the affair at Monreal, broke into open mutiny a few days afterwards. Some of them raised cries in favour of Don Carlos, others in favour of Don Alfonso; and the majority threw up their caps and shouted enthusiastically for the Republic, meaning always that Federal Republic which they did not understand, and which had not yet been created. The latter demonstration was quite as much a breach of discipline in its way as the others. It was stated that agents of the Carlist party, which was strong in Pampeluna, provoked these disturbances in the first instance, plying the men with liquor, and supplying them with money. At all events, that is how the Government accounts for the outbreak. In their turn the Republicans got excited, and instigated the soldiers to demand that the thirteen Carlist prisoners they had taken should be shot without trial or benefit of clergy, in defiance of the laws of honourable warfare. These Republicans are not scrupulous. They talked of massacring all the Carlist sympathizers in Pampeluna—in short, of commencing a sort of Sicilian Vespers on a smaller scale; and so threatening did their attitude become at one period, that the priests in the town had to disguise themselves as peasants and fly to the mountains, and the laymen who were suspected of a love for Royalty had to block up their doors and windows. This was what one of the few trustworthy journals of Madrid, *El Imparcial,* related, and may account for the inactivity of the gallant General Nouvilas quite as much as that sore throat which confined him to his room.

In Catalonia the disorganization was worse. The battalion of Chasseurs of Manila separated into several parties, which were wandering over the province, spreading terror wherever they went. The patriotism of the volunteers of the Republic had been invoked to try and bring them back to discipline. Such an attempt might lead to combats that would have the result of embittering still more the spirit of the freebooters, which those soldiers were in the fullest sense of the word. Persuasion by gunpowder, when employed by irregulars, seldom pacifies regulars. Either of two events was possible—those soldiers would get the better of the volunteers, or might turn over to the side of Don Carlos. Meantime the Carlist bands in the province are increasing, and have the field pretty much to themselves. Four hundred officers of the army came to Madrid the other day, and are now walking about the capital *en pékin.* Like the frozen-out gardeners who parade London suburbs in the depth of a hard winter, they've "got no work to do," but, unlike those impostors, they are really anxious for a job. I have chatted with some of those officers, and I know several of them would not be averse to flashing a sword for the son of their former Queen. They had to leave their regiments because they could no longer command them. The bonds of discipline were completely smashed. The men were unmanageable. In some barracks Phrygian caps were as common as the regulation head-gear. The sergeants of the line, jealous of the promotion of the sergeants of the artillery, thought they should have their turn; and the privates did not see the justice of volunteers being offered two pesetas, or about 1s. 7d. a day, while they, who did more and better work, encountered more risks, and suffered more hardships, received but a miserable pittance of a few pence. The general in command was recalled, and Contreras sent down in his place. He has a reputation as an unimpeachable Republican, one of old standing, and not "for this occasion only;" and much faith was reposed in the influence of his name. But Contreras failed to charm; and, indeed, he appears to have gone the wrong way about his business. An officer whom he put under reprimand went to two barracks and tried to rouse the men to mutiny. He failed; but the men were so little careful of discipline that they let him depart in peace. At last two adjutants on the personal staff of Contreras arrested him and brought him before the General. What course did the General, whose authority had been thus grossly set at defiance, adopt? Order the offender to be shot? No. That would be the mode in a serious army. But Contreras is not Suwarrow. He dismissed the mutineer in epaulettes with a fatherly admonition—appealed to his better feelings. In all likelihood, General Contreras felt that he could not afford to be justly severe. The army was too restive.

Private letters from Barcelona do not mince the matter. The few columns which went out against the Carlists refused to march unless they were headed by detachments of Republican volunteers. The officers ran serious personal risks in their quarters. One of them was condemned to death by a mock court-martial of his own men, and was actually put on his knees preliminary to being shot, when a sergeant interposed, and harangued his comrades into moderation. But all the sergeants have not the good sense and courage of that worthy fellow. Some privates in Barcelona have been trying to have their own profit out of the Republic, by discharging themselves from further service without as much as asking leave; they have sold their uniforms to the dealers in old clo', and are going about the streets in peasant dress, making no secret of their intention to give up the trade of fighting. The great anxiety of the Republican man-at-arms in Spain is to turn his sword-bayonet into a sickle, and his rifle into a mattock. That is what he pretends; I hope he has not a sly hope of vegetating for the rest of his days in lazy vagabondage, with occasional spasms of brigandage just to keep his hand in at shooting. A training in the Spanish army is not exactly the thing to fit for the peaceful and toilsome monotony of industrial occupations.

The battalions of cazadores of Mérida and Barcelona, in garrison at Valencia, exhibited symptoms of discontent; but the officers were on the alert, and checked them on the spot. That is the only plan—nip the evil in the bud. It is the custom in Spain to confine troops to barracks during times of popular commotion. The artillery quartered at Valladolid caught the contagion of mutiny, and would have broken their bounds but for the prompt arrival of the captain-general and military governor, who succeeded with some trouble in pacifying them. These unpleasant tokens are not confined to the land forces; they are said to have spread to the sailors and marines. A steamer was under orders to leave the port of Barcelona the other night, but the crew emphatically refused to go; they argued that they were entitled to be paid off, and enjoy liberty on shore, under the benign regulations of the Republic. To be brutally candid, the army has taken the bit between its teeth and bolted. I fear I am repeating a twice-told tale, but it is well that it should be impressed on the reader, that he may know what the cuckoo-cry of "No army" signifies. One of the leading points of the programme of the Spanish Republicans out of office was that a soldier was a machine, and that no soldier should exist in a free nation. Now that the Republicans are in office the soldiers take them at their word, and claim their discharges. The machinery is out of gear. The Republicans never contemplated that they would require soldiers to put down a civil war. Señor Figueras, in spite of all his eloquence and honesty, can hardly be more successful in pacifying turbulent Barcelona than General Contreras. Catalonia is as great a stickler for its usages as the Basque provinces are for their fueros. One of the fueros of the Basque provinces is exemption from the quinta, or conscription; their only soldiers are the Miqueletes, a body of men somewhat like the Irish constabulary, who are not bound to act beyond their own provinces. Thus the army which is serving against the Carlists in Biscay, Alava, and Guipúzcoa, is in the provinces, but not of them. Catalonia cries out against the conscription, too, and Barcelona—hot-blooded, troublesome Barcelona, which never loses a chance of standing up for independent opinions—encouraged her garrison in the demand for its discharge.

The regular troops were to be replaced by the highly-paid volunteers. That was the proposition. But how is the increased call on the Financial Ministry to be met? Where is the money to pay these volunteers to come from? And without regular troops, what was to become of Cuba? The gold that is brought back from the Pearl of the Antilles is dearly bought with Spanish blood. People in England little dream what a drain that everlasting little-thought-of Cuban insurrection was upon the Spanish army. Thousands of men perished in the island every year, not from the bullets of the insurgents, but from privations, fatigue, the torrid clime, and the deadly swamp fever.

In sum, the army has been petted; the army is spoiled; the army, like a wanton child, is naughty. Ministers have shown indecision in shifting generals, generals have set the example of indiscipline in tolerating mutinous officers, officers have thrown off their uniforms in dudgeon and despair, sergeants have waylaid the War Office, so to speak, with the cry of "Promotion or your life!" Can poor Pistolet of the rank and file be blamed if he sighs for freedom, his sweetheart, and his native village? The Republic promised him all these, and now he is wicked enough to ask for them. There is one way of bringing naughty children to their senses, but Pistolet is too big a boy to submit to the rod from a weakly master.

In the capital we were comparatively safe. Unless the garrison divided against itself or the ordinary troops and the Guardia Civil fell out, there was no danger of bloodshed in any quantity. The population is not singularly ferocious. The privates move quietly in the streets in pairs, and are particular to salute their officers, though there is one officer, on an average, to every fifteen men, and most of these officers lack the thoroughbred air of gentlemen, and apparently have risen from a low social level. The sergeants are self-controlled, and brighten the promenades with their green worsted gloves and the great laced V's on their sleeves. I never miss a chance of admiring the garrison at parade. Physically the men are up to a high standard—superior to those of most European armies; morally they have the name of being patient and well-conducted; in formation they are steady, in dressing precise, and in movement they have a step as quick, but more *dégagé* than the Prussians. Were I a Spaniard, I would, every time I bent in prayer, offer up a supplication for the conversion—or perhaps the something else— of the bedizened culprits who are sending the soldiers to rack and ruin.

CHAPTER XII.

Luring the Reader into a Stony Desert—A Duel on the Carpet— Disappointment of the Special Correspondents—The People Amuses Itself—How the Ballot Works—A Historic Sitting of the Congress— Castelar's Great Oration—The Glory of Spain—About Negro Manumission—Distrust of "Uncle Sam"—Return of Figueras—The Permanent Committee—A Love-Feast of Politicians—The Writer Orders Wings.

IT may be urged with some show of truth that under the mirage of the adventurous, I have lured the reader, anxious for the sensational, into exhausting deviations in the stony desert of politics. I am guilty, and I am sorry that I shall have to sin again—politics are so ultimately interwoven with life in Spain. But it must not be imagined that these accounts of what happened more than a decade ago are no more useful or interesting than the stale report of the death of Queen Anne. In Spain history has the trick of literally repeating itself. The country is split into the same camps still, and occurrences similar to those of which I treat are certain to be presented to the world anew. The drama will be the same; the company only will be strange. And the information, such as it is, which I give now, may furnish the key to much that would otherwise be hard to unlock when the curtain rings up again.

Before one more error of political errantry, I must tell of a duel which did not come off, for the sake of its moral. This was how the affair arose. There was a discussion in the Assembly in reference to an alleged insurrection in Porto Rico. Señor Padial asked, was it true that the insurgents had raised cries of "Death to Spain," and demanded the independence of Porto Rico, and the massacre of the local volunteers? Several members got up to speak, and one of them, for what reason I cannot fathom, characterized the question as "a farce unworthy of the Conservative party." After a little while Señor Ardanay proceeded to read some documents proving the reality of the disturbances. He was interrupted by a torrent of voices, and Señor Padial shouted that the Civil Guards and volunteers of the island had got up the whole row, and that General Sanz was the author of the farce. General Sanz politely retorted, "Your worship is wanting in truth." Several honourable gentlemen sprang to their feet, and asked that Señor Padial's words should be taken down in writing. And then the Assembly became a bear-garden. Señor Olavarrieta claimed "la palabra," but the President would not give him the privilege of speaking. He spoke all the same, and said, "We shall not allow ourselves to be insulted by those señores," pointing to the Porto Rico deputies. The confusion became worse confounded. The President rang his bell, called "Order," and threatened to suspend the sitting. General Sanz then rose, looking wicked, and asked that the words offensive to the Civil Guards and the volunteers should be taken down in writing. As for what had been said offensive to himself, he asked nothing; he knew what course to take. In England this might have meant that the soldier would treat Señor Padial with silent contempt; in Spain, with my preconceived notions of the pride of blue blood and the fire of Castile, and all the rest, I took it that it could only mean "pistols for two and coffee for one." The confession is sad; but the truth at any price, the truth is so rare under this sky. Sundry Special Correspondents who had come out to describe the revolution that would not come off, were cudgelling their brains to discover how they could assist at this passage of arms, in order that they might render a full, true, and particular account to the public. The encounter would have been more diverting than a bull-fight. Opinions were divided as to whether it was better to go disguised as a hackney coachman or an apothecary's assistant. I hurried, after dinner, to the Café Fornos, the great rendezvous of Madrid politicians, to hear the latest details of the pending affair of honour. It was to come off—no doubt of it; but when and where, I could not hear. Next morning I read that the difficulty had been arranged. It may be a satisfaction that the barbarous "code of honour" has fallen out of fashion in Spain; but it would be a still greater satisfaction if the practice of gentlemen giving each other the lie in public were to fall out of fashion also. The scene was disgraceful, and I am glad to be able to add that most of the deputies were thoroughly ashamed of it; and in places of public resort some went so far as to say that they would take their seats no more in the Assembly. But they were in their places all the same on the following afternoon. The Congress of Spain is no more mannerly on occasions than legislatures elsewhere; but the occasions are rare.

My visit to the Café Fornos was not for nothing, after all. There was a scene there too. A group of low fellows, overheated with wine, entered about eight o'clock, while the immense hall on the ground-floor was crowded with Radical deputies, officers, and quiet Madrileños who frequent it nightly, and commenced bellowing for the Republic after their hearts—that is to say, the Republic, Federal, Social, and Uncompromising. The shout was taken up by another group outside, which blocked up the entrance in the Calle de Alcalá. It was evidently a premeditated manifestation. A Republican deputy who was present tried to calm the disorderly crew, but to no purpose. They had come to shout, and they would have their shout out. Señor Estévanez, the civil governor, was dining in a room upstairs, but Señor Estévanez did not leave his repast. When the thirsty and uncompromising federal social citizens were hoarse they retired. They had effectually succeeded in annoying the coffee-drinking tyrants who had the impudence to wear broadcloth, and they withdrew to drain bumpers to their tremendous exploit elsewhere.

These individuals were all in favour of the "social liquidation." This cry of the drones had partisans in every citizen with an empty pocket and a patch on his garments, for it means that the provident shall be robbed to satisfy the improvident. But nathless these agitators, Spain, I was told, was likely to be quiet for five or six weeks—that is, quiet in the Spanish sense, with an insurrection in one stage of heat or another, smouldering or flaming, in half a dozen provinces. The elections would be tranquil, with "scrimmages" here and there; they would not be elections without. The voting is by ballot. Theoretically the system is faultless, but in practice jugglery is possible, and does habitually occur. The alcalde has some influence in the matter, so has the parish priest, so has the nearest large landed proprietor, so has the local police functionary, and so has the mob. Ballot-boxes have been broken open or have disappeared mysteriously. And thus it happens that a Spanish constituency sends in a buff man as its representative by a crushing majority at one election, and a blue man or a red man by a crushing majority at the next. The constituency has not changed in the interval, but the Minister in the Gobernacion, or, as we should call it, the Home Office, has. There lies the secret.

I pass over small squabbles, which were of daily occurrence at the Palace of the Congress, to come to the sitting of the 21st March, 1873, which deserves to be handed down to history. On that day the Bill for the Abolition of Slavery in Porto Rico was introduced by Castelar, in a speech over which all Madrid went into raptures. The "inimitable tribune," as his admirers call him, surpassed himself. He led off in the usual oratorical style by pretending that he was not going to be oratorical—"the bench on which he sat was one for actions, not words"—and then, in the usual oratorical style, he contrived to say so many words that the official paper next morning was full of them.

His first speech, made when he was but twenty-one, in the year 1854, was on the very same subject, as he reminded his hearers. The Christian religion, he said in the course of his remarks, was the religion of the slave, and the Apocalypse the poem of the slave. Christ was the descendant of enslaved kings, a bondsman of Roman conquerors. But I must give up the attempt to follow the "inimitable tribune;" his lengthened and dazzling chain of eloquence was too elaborate to be picked up link by link. He was historical, passionate, and poetical by turns, but always intensely rhetorical, keeping a close watchfulness for effect, for Señor Castelar does not argue so much as declaim. He had the good taste to defend the Radical Ministry from the charge of having acted in favour of emancipation because the influence of the United States was brought to bear upon it. Such a course, he asserted, would be unworthy of the dignity and independence of the country.

I must tell you that the way to make Spain recoil from doing an act she admits to be good and needful is to counsel her to do it—she will not be advised by others. It would not be Spanish. If a Spaniard has a notion of getting himself re-vaccinated, take care, if you are a friend of his, how you talk to him on the subject. If you recommend him to have the operation performed, he will change his mind at once. He will not be bidden, he will risk small-pox in preference. It may happen that he will die, but at all events he will have the satisfaction of having had his own way.

Señor Castelar flattered the self-love of his countrymen by assuring them that they were magnanimous of their own free will, and not because foreigners had advised them to be magnanimous. He next delivered himself of some tuneful periods about humanity, and then wandered off into a spoken essay on the behaviour of the great European Powers on this question of serfdom. He alluded to England as "the least democratic, but most liberal of nations," and praised Russia for having set Spain the example of unriveting the shackles of the slave. He apostrophized the opponents of abolition, telling them that on their heads would fall the responsibility if the law were not passed, but that he and his colleagues would be answerable for the consequences if the law were passed. Then the speaker waxed patriotic, and spoke the stereotyped sentences on the glory and grandeur of Spain. Why should there be rivalries between Creoles and Peninsulars—those who were born in the colonies and those who were born in the mother-country? It was deplorable. Were they not all of the same race? Was not the blood of the Cid and of Pelayo careering in all their noble veins, and the spirit of Spain living in all their generous souls? His peroration was grandiloquent; he appealed to them to cease their bickerings, to close up their ranks, and to labour unitedly for the maintenance of order, authority, and the integrity of the territory, and they would earn the benediction of history and of conscience, which was much more, for it was the benediction of God.

At the close of his discourse, which was incontrovertibly a masterpiece, Señor Castelar was surrounded by numerous colleagues, and warmly congratulated. His speech established among other welcome things that the orator-minister was no atheist. His remarks breathed the truest Christianity. Next it was manifest that Spain, Republican as Monarchical, would not, without a bitter struggle, cede one inch of territory over which the national flag floated. Those who were interested in the retention of slavery in the colonies were the holders of slave property, and the deputies who had lived there and shaken the pagoda-tree to some purpose, and who, now that they were back in Spain, had a grateful recollection of what they owed to slavery. Those gentlemen predicted that the immediate emancipation of the negro would be the ruin of the colonies, and would inevitably lead to their loss by the mother-country. The Ministry of King Amadeus originally brought in the measure for the abolition of slavery in Porto Rico, preliminary to the introduction of another to get rid of the system in Cuba. The chief argument against the measure was that it was due to intriguing on the part of American politicians, whose object was to smooth the way to the ultimate incorporation of the Antilles with the United States. The sincerity of American friendship is suspected by Spaniards. They know that Uncle Sam has a longing eye on the islands in the Caribbean Sea; and has already tried to negotiate Spain out of her American possessions. Spain, recollecting this keenly, mistrusts him. And Señor Castelar, whilst acquitting his predecessors in office of having acted at the suggestion of the United States, let it be very plainly understood that this Republic would fight that other and greater and aggrandizing Republic to her last man and last dollar, before she would consent to the abandonment of one square foot of soil. The vested rights of slave-owners would not suffer completely, for the bill embraced a proposition to pay them an indemnity equivalent to eighty per cent. of the value of their live chattels. Forty per cent. of this was to be guaranteed by the mother-country, and forty by the enfranchised colony, so that twenty per cent. was the comparatively small pecuniary sacrifice the inheritors of an odious system would have to make to conscience.

Whether the manumission of the bondsman in Cuba, which was bound to come, would hasten the independence of that island—or, what was more likely, its annexation to the United States—I am not competent to pronounce. Ultimately, it is the conviction of the wise and experienced that the Queen of the Antilles must achieve her independence; but it will be less on account of abolition than for reasons geographical, climatic, and military. The ocean rolls between Spain and the sunny cluster of isles, the climate is deadly to the Spanish soldier, and the Spanish army cannot afford a perpetual depletion.

Nobody in Spain dares to defend slavery as moral, or protest against its abolition on grounds higher than those of political expediency. The adversaries of the bill affirmed that gradual abolition would be safer than immediate abolition, and that the matter could well afford to wait. The newly-proclaimed Republic had interests of far greater present importance to attend to, they said; but the philo-negrists retorted that it was a shame not to free the negro under the Republic, which was based on the broad principle of freedom to all, without distinction of colour, and that a beneficent and noble act could not be done too soon. If the Monarchy had lasted, there could be no denying it, this project of abolition would have been enacted without fail.

Late in the night, after Castelar had delivered his oration, Señor Figueras returned from his trip to the provinces. He was met at the railway-station by groups of friends, personal and political, and escorted to his residence, where he was serenaded by the band of a regiment of foot artillery. The night was dark and rainy, which was an ingratitude to the patriotism of the musicians. If it did not savour of ill-nature one might be permitted to remark that speeches, however splendid as specimens of composition from a bench, which the speaker admits should be one for acts, not words, and midnight clangours of a brass band under the dripping window-sills of a tired Minister, were hardly what was needed most and first in the country. But Spain is not like any place else.

On the 22nd the Assembly sat until seven, when there was a break-up of two hours for refreshments; after which was held a night sitting (a most unusual thing), prolonged until half-past one the next morning. This was the last of that Assembly. The powers of the Cortes, save and excepting such as were purely legislative, were delegated to a Permanent Committee of twenty, which was to aid Ministers in their task, until the meeting of the Constituent Cortes. In the interval between the two sittings this committee was chosen by the nominating sections of the Radical and Republican parties respectively, all shades of opinion being represented upon it. The President of the Assembly, the four Vice-Presidents, and the four Secretaries, held *ex-officio* seats on the board. An analysis of the names of the twenty-nine shows that there were fourteen Radicals, eight Federals, four Conciliadores (who may be counted with the Federals), two Conservatives, and an Alfonsist.

This moribund sitting was unique in its unanimity and enthusiasm. The Bill for the Abolition of Slavery in Porto Rico was passed without a dissentient voice. There was kissing and clasping of hands, and friendly hugging all round. Señor Padial and General Sanz, who were anxious to fight a duel to the death a few days before, met in the Salon de Conferencias and made up their quarrel. They cemented their reconciliation with an embrace, and one sentimental Deputy who was looking on, cried, "May this be an auspicious omen of the union between Spain and the Antilles!" Señor Figueras promised that the Executive Power would faithfully see to the maintenance of order during the elections. Another señor proposed that the act they had accomplished on the date of the 23rd should be recorded on a marble tablet, to be erected in the chamber. The proposition was received with cheers; and truly the act which knocked the chains off the limbs of 35,000 slaves merited record. The Marquis of Sardoal, who occupied the presidential throne, prayed God to enlighten the minds of the Government and the Permanent Committee, and then declared the Assembly dissolved. There were loud shouts for the "Federal Republic," and just one weak voice for the "Spanish Republic."

The clouds had blown over. Now was the hour for congratulations. Many persons who were preparing to send away their families resolved to let them remain. I had no further occupation in Madrid. A Deputy who had thirty years' experience of life in the capital told me that this was the last place in Spain where there was likely to be a disturbance for the present; but he added, "If you think of going elsewhere, be sure to give me an address where I can telegraph to you, for something may always turn up." I had waited nigh five weeks in the expectation of that something turning up, and at length I began to think I had better seek fresh fields and take a look at real Spain.

CHAPTER XIII.

The Writer Turns Churlish and Quits Madrid—Sleep under
Difficulties—A Bad Dream—Santa Cruz again—Off St. Helena!—
Dissertation on Stomach Matters—A Hint to British Railway
Directors—"Odds, Hilts and Blades"—A Delicate Little Gentleman is
Curious—The "Tierra Deleitosa"—That Butcher again.

"IF you want to see real Spain," said the British Minister to me, "don't stop
here longer than you can help. Go south." That fixed me. With a natural
impulsiveness I pronounced "the imperial and crowned, very noble and very
loyal and very heroic town"—all which titles it bears—a fraud and a failure
as far as my calling was concerned. There had been great cry and little wool.
I was as churlish as a hangman cheated of his client. That terrible thing which
was perpetually on the eve of coming to pass had not come to pass. After all,
I reflected, it was for the better; for if there had been stupendous tidings to
wire, the Government telegraphic system would have broken down under
the operation. A message more than twenty lines long was a shock to the
clerks, and set them discussing so excitely that they let the fire of their
cigarettes die out. The "only court" grew hateful to my mind. It had produced
no men to charm by, save Frey Lope de Vega Carpio, Don Pedro Calderon
de la Barca, and the Maestro Tirso de Molina—and they were dead. It was a
nest of political hornets, and head-quarters of hyperbole; flimsy feathers of
lying gossip floated thick as midges in midsummer air; as in Athens, the
populace spent its leisure, which was the best part of its life, in nothing but
hearing or telling new stories. I would shake the dust of the Prado off my
feet, in testimony against the unsatisfying capital. Architecturally, it was a
higgledy-piggledy of houses on a high bare site; climatically, it was a mixture
of furnace and hall of winds; socially, it was slow, and a disappointment;
intellectually, it was below zero. My parting words—I cannot say my
farewell—will be framed on those of Jugurtha to Rome: "*Urbem venalem et
mature perituram, si emtorem invenerit.*"

I paid a good-bye visit, with thoughts of a stirrup-cup, to Maceehan, at the
Fornos, and discovered him listening to Bret Harte's poem of "Table
Mountain," recited by Russell Young, who was lolling on a sofa in an upstairs
cabinet. The dentist did not seem to "take much stock in it." An appreciation
of the horrors of Chinese cheap labour requires a liberal antecedent
education on the Pacific slope. Dr. Maceehan was, for his own sake, sincerely
sorry I was going away; but for my sake he was glad, as I had been
overworking myself, and was badly in want of a kick in the liver.

It is an error to speak of any city or people when you are under the influence
of sluggish bile, for you are liable to do them injustice. It is a sin not to

withdraw the unjust words. I am tempted to sin; but on consideration I follow the example familiar in a certain legislature, and take back the unparliamentary language into which I have been betrayed by jecoral derangement. Honour to the manes of Uxem-Ali-Beck, Ambassador from the Shah of Persia, who came to Madrid in 1601, and fell in love there. He liked it. I fell in love ten times a day, but nobody would fall in love with me.

On a Sunday night at nine o'clock, I quitted the city, and on Tuesday morning I had my hair trimmed by a barber of Seville. The journey, like most long railway journeys, is one of infinite weariness to the flesh. The first-class carriages are roomy and well-padded, so that short travelling, except for invalids, is comfortable enough. The correo, or mail train—that which I took—leaves but once in twenty-four hours, and, in consequence of carrying the mails, has to stop at every station, so that its progress is slow, albeit the quickest to be had for money. There were nine sociable young Spaniards in the compartment with me. The gauge of the road is wide, admitting of five broad seats at each side, and the motion of the train is easy and nurses to sleep, without that violent rocking which one sometimes experiences while rattling northwards from London in the Flying Scotchman. But the backs of the seats are stiff and straight as a Prussian drill-sergeant, and do not nurse, but "murder sleep," as I speedily found to my sorrow. However, they do nurse a crick in the neck. I was woke out of a wayward doze just as I was about to undergo the punishment of death by the garrote. I had been dreaming a fearsome dream. In a weak moment I had accepted the crown of Spain. I had granted my subjects every conceivable privilege, pandered to all their crazes, gone so far as to give them a bull-fight every day in the week and two on Sundays and festivals, paying all expenses out of my own royal pockets. But they were not to be satisfied, unless I would go into the bull-ring myself. That was the straw that breaks the camel's back. I flatly refused. They rebelled, kicked me off the throne, led me in a felon's yellow coat on a wretched donkey to the place of execution, and planted me in the fatal chair. Most poignant humiliation yet, all the crowned heads of Europe, led by the Czar of Russia, were invited to the spectacle and joined in a howling chorus of "Serve him right." I looked my last around, and woke up with a toss of my noddle against the back of the seat. We were at Alcázar. A fellow-traveller kindly offered to let me lay my head between his legs if I would give him my carpet-bag for a pillow. There is nothing like reciprocal accommodation on a journey. I agreed, the train started again, and I lost myself in the land of Nod. This time I was following the campaign against the Carlists. Suddenly I was roused by a cry—

"Santa Cruz!"

I knuckled my eyes, the carriage was motionless, and I distinctly heard the name of the dreaded priest Santa Cruz repeated. This was no dream. Had I mistaken the terminus? Had I been speeding northwards all this time? I was in a most perplexed tangle of mind, half pleased at the prospect of meeting the redoubtable Cura in person, half apprehensive lest I might give lodging to a chance bullet, and miss the opportunity of describing him. As I was preparing to jump out, the tram moved on anew. I turned to the railway guide and discovered the explanation of the mystery. Santa Cruz is a station on the Andalusian line between Val de Peñas and Almuradiel. A third time I fell asleep, to be roused by another cry—

"St. Helena!"

Taught by former experience, I was not to be discomposed now. We had pierced the bowels of the Sierra Morena, and Santa Elena was but the name of a station on its southern side. The next time I fell off I enjoyed a genuine sleep. I do not think it would have roused me if "Salt Lake" or "Skibbereen" had been shouted in my ear through a speaking-trumpet.

At Menjibar, where we arrived about ten in the morning, there was a delay of twenty minutes for breakfast. By way of whet, I presume, my fellow-travellers all lit cigarettes as we were gliding up by the platform. This Spanish railway restaurant was a reproach to Mugby Junction. It was scrupulously clean, the fare was excellent, and the tariff moderate. The price of every article was legibly painted in distemper on the walls. Premising that a real is, roundly speaking, twopence halfpenny of our money, a list of some of the viands and liquids to be had and their cost will be interesting—only the reader is requested not to open the book previous to bolting his food at the hurry-up and grab-all refreshment-room at Amiens, or when he is about to confront scalding soup and monumental sandwiches at some of our British buffets. It might ruffle his temper and jeopardize his digestion. A breakfast consisting of a couple of eggs, two plates of meat or fish, dessert, bread and wine, can be had for twelve reals. The wine is the common wine of the country, and pleasant and healthy tipple it is when you get used to it. You can procure a baby bottle full for one real, and if you like to be extravagant you can pay twenty-four for a bottle of Bordeaux, or forty for a bottle of champagne. The Bordeaux is too dear. As for champagne, nobody drinks that habitually except kings of the Bonanza dynasty; but myriads of men, especially at race-meetings, drink a beverage which they take for the bubbling, roseate, kindling nectar with inspiration in every wavering pearlet. "Fizz," I think they call it. I hope they enjoy it. "Compound of crime at a sovereign a quart" (see James Smith's poems somewhere), I call it. He who quaffs champagne at dinner, save on a foggy day, is unworthy of God's gifts. The proper hour for the absorption of that delicious exhilarant is at eleven in the forenoon, and then but two glasses at the most should be taken. These glasses should not be the absurd shallow lapping-glasses, nor yet the slender stork-glasses, but the goodly tumbler. If it be summer, there should be a lump of ice in the crystal goblet; and the connoisseur will always hold it between him and the sunlight before imbibition, and ejaculate, "There's a picture!" For these hints I am indebted to that princely gourmet of palate most exquisite, John Kavanagh, of the Inman ocean-ferry line, Founder and President of the Cocktail Club, of which I am the Laureate. Returning from our divagation, the amateur of beer may have a big bottle at these Spanish railway hotels for four reals, but I counsel him abstention. It is never advisable to drink beer in a wine-growing country. The soul of Sir Wilfrid Lawson would be elevated to the height of successful joke-making at the catalogue of the teetotal drinks, which range from sugared water to milk and orangeade. My weakness is egg-flip. For dinner, which is to be partaken of at fourteen reals, one has a soup, a fry, an *entrée*, a roast, a salad, two sweets or fruits, bread and wine. The *entrées* are usually rib of mutton, veal or a beefsteak, which sometimes makes you think there is something like leather. A hen, which is a luxury, rates at fourteen reals, but a tortilla of the hen's eggs is to be preferred. If any complaints are felt to be necessary as to attendance or provand, the station-master has a volume wherein to write them down at the disposal of travellers.

From Menjibar we steamed along through a beautiful landscape of this beautiful province of Andalusia. The fields were emerald green and ought to be fertile, but they seemed to lack cultivation. Very few persons were to be seen working in them. In proportion as nature had been prodigal, man appeared to be lazy. Still, viewed as the painter, not the agriculturist would view it, the landscape was delicious in its quiet loveliness. Patches of silvery grey—that dreamy neutral silvery grey which is to be caught in perfection on willows played upon by moonlight—here and there lightened the mellow masses of verdure. Those were olive groves. The hills on the horizon, seen through an odd curtain of rain, for the day was showery, had the vaporous hazy outline of some of Murillo's pictures. Anon we passed by the bridge of Alcolea, the scene of the defeat of Queen Isabella's forces under Nouvaliches by Serrano in 1868. The field is altogether too pretty to have been defiled by a sanguinary episode of civil war. A gently winding stream courses 'mid rich undulating meadows at the base of a ridge of hills covered with cottages enbowered in plantations and orchards. As if inflamed by the warlike associations of the locality, my companions produced sword-canes, dirks and poniards, and began comparing them with the air of experts. Not one of these sociable young Spaniards was unprovided with a lethal weapon. I was devoutly thankful that they had not got to talking politics on the road, or I might have had to deplore the absence of a bye-law applying to passengers carrying edged tools from that code which so carefully shuts out the drunkard, and insists that nobody with a loaded gun or pistol shall enter a carriage.

At Córdoba the train stopped, and we changed carriages for the Andalusian capital. During my short stay I was invited to take my choice of a varied assortment of daggers, navajas, skeens, and stylets, which a sturdy hawker, who looked as if he knew how to handle them, had strung round his waist.

The fellow was a perfect walking arsenal, or rather a peripatetic bit of Sheffield, and expatiated affectionately on the temper and cutting qualities of his wares. I declined to buy. He showed his teeth, and told me I might go farther and fare worse. I was very happy to take him at his word, and get into a carriage that was going as far as Seville, which was occupied by only one person, a delicate little gentleman with a bright, keen, kindly face. To him came a courier as he leant out of the carriage-window.

"Why does one see so many Scotch caps about?" asked the little gentleman, in English.

"Because Gibraltar is near, and there are smugglers there," answered the courier.

"Why does one see so many dogs about?" asked the little gentleman.

"Because they find more food here than at home," answered the courier.

"Why does not one see the train start to time?" asked the little gentleman.

"Because this is Spain," answered the courier.

That was conclusive, and the little gentleman drew in his head and sat down opposite me. He was a charming companion, a young American of culture and courtly manners, who was travelling in Spain for his health. He loved the country and the people, and told me many anecdotes of acts of kindness of which, being sickly, he had been the object from this strange, tender, passionate race, as ready with generous help as with the stiletto-point. Poor little gentleman! I fear he has made a void in some fond household long since, for he was sore stricken with decline.

"The Spaniard," he said, "in fine, is the most courteous of men; he never sits down to eat in your presence without offering you a share of his meal." And it is true.

From Córdoba to Seville the way lies through a land of delights—the "tierra deleitosa" of Andalusia. Again we swept by green fields and silvery grey olive groves; anon we skirted vivid clusters of orange-trees laden with the great luscious fruit, which is ever in season. On we passed by plains bristling with huge spiky clumps of aloes alternating with growths of Barbary figs, until, towards twilight, we came in sight of the Guadalquivir with its boats, and on the farther side, near a copse of cypress, the walls of the Cartuja Convent, now turned into a porcelain factory by an enterprising Englishman, who makes imitation Moorish tiles where the hooded friars sang matins and lauds.

It was seven o'clock when we drove into "proud Seville," too late to look at any of her marvels, but not too late to enjoy a good dinner in the Fonda de Paris, a namesake and branch of the hotel where I had been stopping at Madrid. My *vis-à-vis* at the dinner-table was the Saragossa butcher—I began to think now he was a political agent—who had been my *vis-à-vis* on my tedious ride over the mountains from Beasain to Alsasua. Was this varlet on my track? I began to entertain serious apprehensions on the score. It has been my lot for years to have been shadowed by *mouchards*, gendarmes, detectives, and policemen.

My goings-out and my comings-in have been noted; my house has been watched by hulking louts in uniform whom their foolish superiors pitched upon as accomplished pryers; nay, even a female with *pince-nez*, sealskin jacket, long purse, and an Ollendorffian intimacy with most Continental tongues, has been cunningly slipped at my heels. I have been, thank the Lord, misunderstood by fools, belied by knaves, avoided by the timorous, tabooed by the contemptibly "respectable" (odious word), and slandered by scoundrels whom I had befriended. Heads have been wagged, and I have been adjudged a deep card and a dangerous character. Nothing could be got out of *me*.

The explanation is simple. I had nothing to conceal. You cannot squeeze aqua tofana out of a stone. I was suspected, I take it now, because, in the exercise of my vocation, I had been thrown into the society of Communists, Nihilists, Fenians, and Carbonari. Had I confined myself to card-sharpers, prize-fighters, copper captains, hypocrites, libertines, and ladies of the Loosened Cincture, all would have been well. And yet, 'fore Heaven, I can assure the Powers, great and small, I have never meditated wrong to a State or a potentate, never harboured an unkind thought for a dog, and never joined a secret society but the Order of Antediluvian Buffaloes, and they expelled me from the lodge for unbuffalo-like behaviour.

If I was sure that Saragossa butcher was a spy, I would not put prussic acid in his chocolate, but I almost think I would sprinkle cowhage between his sheets.

CHAPTER XIV.

Delectable Seville—Don Juan Scapegrace—The Women in Black—In the Triana Suburb—The City of the Seven Sleepers—Guide-Book Boredom—Romance and Reality—The Prosaic Manchester Man— King Ferdinand Puzzling the Judges—Mortification by Proxy—Some Notable Treasures—Papers and Politics—The Porcelain Factory— "The Lazy Andalusiennes"—About Cigars—The Gipsy Dance.

THERE are but three spots in the world of which I had formed mental pictures from my reading, that rose to the level of anticipation when I came to visit them. Venice was one of these, Naples another, and Seville, delectable Seville, the third. There is a Spanish proverb which declares, "Who hath not seen Seville hath not seen a marvel," and I am prepared to own that who doth not believe that proverb is an unenviable sceptic. At first sight the city is a disappointment. Glance at it from the railway and you will have no wish to stop. But alight and remain there a few days, and you will find it hard to drag yourself away. The place grows upon you. Each hour reveals new charms; there is a fascination in the very atmosphere; and in the end you will catch yourself exclaiming that the pearl of Andalusia is the fairest gem in the Spanish crown—would be a priceless ornament to any crown.

The setting of the jewel is not worthy of it—a great plain covered with greyish grass; clumps of tall, brown-blossomed agave; a sky metallic in its lustre, blazing and intense; a dim streak of azure on the horizon indicating the far sierra, and, creeping lazily through the flat, a dull, yellow river. But the city itself! Verily, it is a marvel—a grotto of serene mysteries in a granary of plenty, the true city to cultivate the gay science and savour the delicate relishes of bliss.

Don Juan—I mean the Don Juan of the Tenorio family, linked to fame by Tirso de Molina, Glück, and Mozart, not the hero of Byron's poem—was born here, lived here, and lies under an ivy-clad sarcophagus in the gardens attached to the Duke de Monpensier's palace. No sweeter nook of earth could he have chosen for life's dreary pilgrimage, which he made as little dreary as he well could, if one-half that is said and sung of him be true. He was a sad scapegrace, and no pattern to the rising generation; his back knew no sackcloth, and his shoes no peas; but he died penitent. His tomb, a chaste thing in marble and brass, ought to be as attractive for pilgrims of the Wertherian school as the monument to Abélard in the Père-la-Chaise.

Threading the puzzling maze of Seville streets, one might fancy that all the ladies here had been in love with the wanton rascal, and were still in mourning for him. The dress of womankind of the better class is invariably black; their tiny feet, coffined in dainty shoes, peep from under a pall of black skirts;

black mantillas float over billows of inky hair, while black eyes flash with the melancholy fire of funeral torches over the tremulous tips of black fans. Why they patronize black (which is a conductor of heat) in this hot climate I cannot for the life of me make out. Certainly it is not because of sympathies solemn or lugubrious; for the character of these lissom damsels of Seville is the reverse of gloomy. There is no taint of Inquisitorial days in their souls. They are grave only externally, and all that is coquettish, winning, and womanly within. If they hang out the undertaker's emblems it can only be through love of the rule of contraries, for they are arch in every step and glance, and bring sunshine with them into shady places. They are fond of seeing and being seen; they cannot be looked on as mutes, for they carry a fan, which in Spain is equivalent to a semaphore; why then will they persevere in wearing this sepulchral raiment? I flatter myself I have discovered two reasons, either of which will answer—first, to typify their remorse for all the hearts they have broken; and, next, because it is very becoming.

The women of the lower classes do not confine themselves to the same severity of taste. They are as amorous of glaring colours as negresses. Cross the iron bridge over the Guadalquivir, here a slow current of chocolate and milk, and go into the Triana suburb where Tatterdemalion holds court. There you will meet gowns of printed cotton of the liveliest hue—gowns that flaunt violent pinks and gamboges, but never a violet or a pearl-grey, much less a black. These daughters of the people generally adorn their braided dark hair, which is thick and silky enough to drive a Parisian belle into agonies of jealousy, with a few bright natural flowers, and sport cheap trinkets and ear-rings, and fling gay kerchiefs over their shoulders. The men are as true to the native costume as the women. That abomination, the stove-pipe hat, seldom shocks the æsthetic mind. The head-gear is the wide round hat with low crown and inward-turned brim. The large blue or brown cloak, with parti-coloured lining, is almost universally worn as in Madrid, but with this difference: in Madrid the tail of it is held before the mouth as if there was an epidemic of toothache; in Seville, it drapes full and free. The Andalusian jacket—broidered with tags, and short so as to show the scarlet waist-sash— tight trousers, and shoes of untanned leather, are likewise common. A tidy active working-suit this Andalusian suit is, but it must no more be argued that the men who wear it are tidy and active and addicted to hard work than that the women who wear black are going to a burial-service. No; Seville is the most deliciously idle place in creation, and the Sevillanos are the most deliciously idle people.

The *vis inertiæ* is cultivated here as a science; the Castle of Indolence is somewhere in the vicinity; the central offices of the Lazy Society are situated in the Calle de las Sierpes. The natives take to lotus-eating naturally. Pure effect of climate. The Seven Sleepers were born in Seville, and their descendants still have their torpid being in the city. It was never meant for the bustle of trade or the whirr of machinery. It is the place of all others to read Theocritus, 'mid bowers dipping their leaves into plashing fountains, to eat fruit, listen to distant music, blow languid wreaths of perfumed smoke, and shut one's eyes to have visions of fair women. It is the veritable opium-eater's Paradise.

Of deliberate design, I abstain from writing of the public buildings and monumental curiosities of Seville. All that can be had by those who choose in the exhaustive guide-books of Richard Ford and Henry O'Shea. To my thinking, nothing can be more insufferable than the statistics of architecture, the bald jargon of styles plateresque and ornaments charrigueresque, the raptures over chancels and transepts and ogee windows, the precise accounts of such a bell, which would turn the scale at so many hundredweight, and such a spire, which is three yards and a quarter taller than the York Column, with the everlasting scraps of poetry from the treasury of ready-made quotations interlarded between. It is worse even than the cant of criticism which Laurence Sterne castigated with honest pen. Hugo was a genius, and even Hugo was almost unequal to saving "Notre Dame de Paris" from the dead weight of architectural detail which cumbered its spirit.

Let us look at Seville without the guide-book or guide, walk through its labyrinth of narrow paved streets with mind open to receive, and mark the features of the East side by side with those of the West. Those flat-roofed buildings with greeneries on the summit, those jealous balconies and windows with their iron trellis-work, those cool inner spaces with tesselated floors and surrounding of marble pillars of which we catch glimpses through the metal fret-work of the private doors—how Moorish they are! The sights and sounds, the ragged and bronzed beggar urchins, the hawkers of lemons and water, the strings of donkeys and mules in fringed blinkers pattering along under huge net or straw panniers, crammed with fruit, or charcoal, or tiles, or cork-wood—how characteristic, how utterly un-Frankish! That lolling clown, with legs dangling over the tawny sheared sides of a diminutive donkey, is a study in himself. Then the melodious street-cries, the lively braying and whinnying, and the perpetual tinkling of the collar-bells worn by all four-footed beasts that pass, except nobody's dog and the rich man's horse—what a pleasant concert they make!

If you wish to change the scene, roam through the plazas, with their marble water-basins and orange-trees; go to the Duke de Montpensier's garden, with its wealth of myrtles and fern palms; wander to the river-side and look at the ships lading or unlading; or ascend the Giralda, the old mosque steeple from which the muezzin called the faithful to prayer, and take in the comely mass of colour beneath in one broad sweep. Then the changing sky that canopies this "fragment of heaven let fall upon earth!" The riot of clouds when the elements war, and after the midday heats the genial rain pours down as if the blue expanse overheard were a lake—how fervent and cordial! At night, when the city streets are crowded with groups in conversation; when the fragrant, flower-garlanded patios are visible by mystic lights pendent from gilt chandeliers, like votive lamps before a shrine; when caballeros pay court to their lady-loves through gratings as caballeros are licensed only to pay court in Spain; when plaintive songs, with a reminiscence of the desert about them, are chanted in monotonous cadence to the accompaniment of a guitar—how grateful it all is to him who is not lost to the sense of poetry! Imperceptibly one yields himself to the associations of the bygone, and imagination takes wing. As the night ages and silence enwraps the scene—a silence only broken by the deep boom from a clock-tower or the voice of the sereno, the Spanish watchman, hobbling along with his lantern swinging from his pike and his bunch of keys from his girdle, singing out the hours—the effect is stronger; and I confess, while roaming in such a frame once, I so lost myself to the present that I should not have been surprised if I had met the Knight of La Mancha and the three gallants of the *Canard à Trois Becs* in mocking whispers at his heels, or Figaro himself on a serenading excursion; but with the last puff of my cigar died out the ideal and returned the real. I hastened back to my hotel, which might once have been a Moorish palace, and there, to make the assurance doubly sure that this was the nineteenth century, sat in an American rocking-chair a gentleman in a tweed suit, reading *Galignani's Messenger* and drinking pale ale.

That gentleman was not a poet; he was an English tourist. It was the period before the Holy Week, with its world-renowned solemnities, celebrated with a pomp second only to that of Rome in her heyday, and drawing strangers in swarms from every point of the compass. If I expected to enjoy an intellectual chat with that gentleman I was mistaken.

"Only fancy!" he began; "the landlord has been here, and the beggar says we'll have to pay double for board and lodging if we don't clear out before the 5th of April."

To my explanation that a time of deep interest was at hand, and that accommodation would be at a premium, Manchester (I felt instinctively he must be a commercial traveller and in the dry-goods line) continued: "Yes, I know: bull-fights, Italian opera at the San Fernando, races, fat women, talking seals, peep-shows, whirligigs—all the fun of the fair. By Jove! I've half a mind to hang on."

He had not heard of the grand open-air religious processions from Palm Sunday to Good Friday, nor of the uniquely pathetic service of the *Tenebræ*, nor of the gorgeous jubilance of Easter Sunday. Some enemy to Seville spread the rumour that the Republic had set its face against such ceremonies as mere gauds and vanities, customs more honoured in the breach than the observance, and that this year they would not be held. But Seville would not have it so; she would not relinquish her chance of enjoying a religious raree-show and fleecing the foreigner for any Republicans. The civil governor issued a proclamation comforting the lieges by the pledge that now, as ever, the Holy Week would be grandly kept, kept in a way worthy of cultured Seville, and cultured Seville rubbed her hands with glee. Crowds were expected to flock in, and the master of the hotel intended to act royally by them—that is, exact tribute from them whilst they were at his mercy. Seville meant to be awfully devout during Passion Week, and awfully jolly the week after. On Easter Sunday there was to be a bull-fight, one of the finest in Spain, between the greatest of living toreadores and some bulls of choicely savage breed. The annual fair, which was represented to me as a revel of glowing and changing tints in dress—a treat not to be missed by the artist on any account—was to be held in the middle of April, and speculative committees were busy over the details of race-meetings, balls, fireworks, and merry-making generally.

I pressed the representative of the mart of cotton not to depart. But he was obdurate to arguments touching on the æsthetic. For him the sacred Biblico-traditional drama of "The Seven Dolours of the Virgin Mary" had no attraction. He preferred fireworks and the learned pig.

"No," he added, as if musing; "on second thought, I shan't. Bull-fights I can see at Madrid; and the only race-meeting worth attending, I'm told, is that at the place where the sherry is manufactured."

"Surely," I ventured, with artless good-nature, "you will wait to patronize Mr. Spiller, who is advertised as skater-in-ordinary to the Duke of Edinburgh. It will be something to boast of, that you saw him gliding and gyrating before the astonished natives, whose only idea of ice is in the shape of creams, dyed a delicate amber, and tinctured with essence of lemon. Then, again, your countryman, old Tom Price, the Batty of the Peninsula, has pitched his tent on the Alameda of Hercules. He's not to be missed."

"Tom Price—bah! You should go to Astley's, in the Westminster Bridge Road, my boy. That fairly takes the cake. I'm off!"

He went, and I was not sorry; but the spell was broken. I was guest of an inn. My elysian train of reverie had been smashed up; the genius of dry-goods had evicted poetry under circumstances of aggravated harshness; before the stamp of the elastic-sided boot of Manchester, Pedro the Cruel and Alonso the Wise, Murillo and Luca Giordano, Maria de Padilla and Leonora de Guzman, "el Rey Chiquito" Boabdil and the heir of Columbus—all had melted into thinnest of air.

Inexorable duty called me elsewhere before the Holy Week solemnities, so that I have no opportunity of describing them *de proprio visu*, and I do not care to rehearse twice-told tales. But whilst I was in Seville I wandered to and fro and made good use of my leisure, hearing and seeing as much as most visitors. Of those things which remain imprinted on my memory I may repeat some without incurring—at least so I trust—the imputation of boring the reader. There was a basin in the gardens of the Alcázar, where I was wont to sit beneath the shade of the foliage in the strong heats of noon. There is an anecdote concerning it which impressed me mightily. King Ferdinand was here one day, and was sore perplexed by an affair of state. He required a just and astute judge to decide some vexed question of the first importance. Walking up and down he unconsciously picked an orange, cut it in twain, and flung one half into the water, the cut side downwards. Suddenly an idea struck him. The monarch sent for a judge, and asked what was that floating before him.

"An orange," was the answer.

Irritated, he dismissed him, summoned another, put the same question, and received the same reply. This went on until at length one authority, before answering, drew the fruit towards him with the branch of a tree, picked it out of the water, and gave the true reply:

"Half an orange!"

There is a sound moral at the core of this orange.

There are five-and-twenty parish churches in Seville and two thousand priests; but, as too often happens on the Continent, the women were vastly more attentive than the men to observances of devotion. I made the acquaintance of a wealthy burgess, a dealer in curiosities, who asked me round to his shop to inspect some of the charming peasant costumes of Murcia, now fast falling into disuse—and a grievous pity it is. It was Friday when I visited him, and he was gobbling pork-chops.

"What! you a Christian, you a son of the Church!" I exclaimed.

"Ah! señor," he apologized; "forgive me! I am very frail, but my wife is *so* good a Christian. I reverence that woman. She has gone to Mass without breaking her fast, and when she returns she will only take one small cup of chocolate."

But all the burgesses of Seville are not like to him who practised mortification by proxy. The gentlefolk are pious, and the commonalty are not irreligious. Cheerfulness and sobriety are the rule; gambling and an idleness excused by the enervating influences of the too generous sun are the predominating vices, as elsewhere in Southern Spain.

I saw few ebullitions of temper, much hospitality among the poor, no downright thievishness, but the irresistible tendency to pass bad money—which is accounted a venial failing in the Peninsula.

The Cathedral is a superb pile, and occupies the site of an ancient mosque. The stained-glass windows are so many captive rainbows. Pretermitting talk about dimensions and the like, I may note some few of the remarkable features which are most apt to be recalled by the stranger. Foremost among these are the stone pulpit from which St. Vincent de Ferrer preached; the slab over the remains of Ferdinand, son of Christopher Columbus, whereon are inscribed the words (referring to his illustrious father), "A Castilla y á Leon Mundo Nuevo Dió Colon," and a Crucifixion by a Mexican negro, who was never known to paint any other subject. It is a peculiarity of artists of the Spanish school, in representations of the Sacrifice on Calvary, to use three nails and place the wound on the right side; Italians use four, and place it on the left. In the Capilla Real is the figure of the "Vírgen de los Reyes," the patron of Seville, a gift from St. Louis of France, surmounted by the identical crown with which the brow of the canonized monarch was pressed, and enclasped as to the throat by a diamond necklace valued at ninety thousand duros, presented by Doña Berenguela, the mother of St. Ferdinand. Among the treasures in the relicario of the sacristy is a massive gold group made of ore brought by Columbus from America, consisting of two figures sustaining a globe, the globe alone weighing fifteen pounds. Passing under a horseshoe arch, in a dusty corridor beside which is preserved the shrivelled mummy of an ungainly alligator sent by the Sultan of Egypt to Alonso the Wise when seeking his daughter's hand, the Chapter Library is reached. The prizes of this collection are the manuscripts of the discoverer of the New World and the book, "*Tractatus de Imagine Mundi,*" which he took with him on the caravel when he first crossed the Atlantic. There are marginal notes to it in his own minute and legible handwriting, in one of which he lays down this apothegm of sad wisdom: "No one is secure from adversity." There are no especially beautiful pictures by Murillo—especially, I say, for all of his are beautiful—in the Cathedral, but the church of La Caridad contains two masterpieces: the "Miracle of our Lord feeding the Multitude," and that of "Moses bringing the Living Water from the Rock of Horeb." The latter is full of diversity of expression underlain by a thrill of mad eagerness brought out with a terrible truth. Another famous picture is the "Descent from the Cross" of Campana. This was painted in 1548, and was so natural that Murillo was never weary of resting in rapt contemplation before it, and on his death-bed asked to be buried at its feet in the church of Santa Cruz. He had his wish. But the dogs of war came panting that way. Soult entered Seville, pulled down the church, desecrated the master's grave, and stole all of his canvas he could lay his sacrilegious paws upon to grace the Louvre. The Spaniards do not love the French, nor is it astonishing.

Among the delights of Seville one of the chief must not fail to be enumerated—no shrieking newsboys shove latest editions into the face of the lounger. This is not a reading people; for a woman to know how to read was accounted immoral so late as the beginning of this century. There are some papers at Seville, nevertheless; among others, *El Oriente*, devoted to Carlism, and *La Legitimidad*, which advocated the interests of the ex-Queen Isabella's son and heir; but they have little to say. In the lack of suicides, stabs in the dark, and pronunciamientos, they are driven to fill up their space with extracts from the almanac and lists of letters thrown into the Post Office without prepayment. Some countryman must have caught the local disease, for in one list given in *La Legitimidad* it was notified that two envelopes had been indolently committed to the box without stamps, one addressed to "Miss Mary, Hyde Park," and the other to "Monsieur" (an evident misprint for "Mister") "Francis O'Mahony, Shankerhill."

It may be a surprise to some that Carlism had its adherents, but wherever the Church is powerful there Carlism exists, and as the Church is particularly powerful amongst the weaker sex, the Spanish women are almost universally Carlists. Many a ferocious Intransigente, who spouts fire and brimstone, and death to kings and priests in the clubs, has to sing very small when he comes home, for the Señora dotes on Don Carlos and works slippers for the father confessor. In Seville I should say the Intransigente element is feeble; it is strongest, perhaps, in the municipality (which, by the way, issued an edict secularizing the cemetery of San Fernando), because this party of action is always on the watch and pushes itself into office; but the immense majority of the business folk are monarchical, only they wish to have the Prince of the Asturias, not Don Carlos, for their monarch, and all the gentlefolk, without exception, are anti-Republican. I had proof of this at the theatre, where "La Marsellesa," a comedy intended to glorify the advent of the Republic, was played. The speeches in favour of Federalism very often fell flat, and occasionally were hissed, while the satirical hits at "social liquidation" and the like were uncommonly relished.

I have dwelt on indolent Seville. Surely there must be some industries pursued in this metropolis of the *dolce far niente*. They are not many.

There is a cannon-foundry and a copper-foundry, but more in keeping with the associations of the radiant district is the porcelain factory. An Englishman, Mr. Charles Pickman, bought one of the convents sequestered in 1836, and has transformed it into a factory, where he turns out some capital imitations of the ancient glazed tiles. Seldom has a hive of industry been reared in nobler building or on more lovely site, nestling in gardens enamelled with flowers, wealthy in fruit-trees, and on the banks of a river. Some may consider it profanity that potters' wheels spin and buzz in an edifice once consecrated to religion; but labour is prayer, and sanctifies of itself. A number of healthy, handsome girls are busily engaged colouring and burnishing the ceramic ware which is fashioned in the old cloisters; and their joyous songs over their work cannot be very displeasing to the spirits of the pious brethren who preceded them in the locality, if there be any ground for the belief that the shades of the dead are permitted to haunt the spots they tenanted in the flesh. There are in those songs reminiscences of Bizet's *Carmen*. These Andalusian lasses have to thank the Englishman for giving them the opportunity of earning their bread and olives honestly, and they have the happy look of independence. Their full-blooded complexions would shame our pale Lancashire factory hands. They can hardly realize how lucky they are to ply such a neat trade in an atmosphere of freshness and sweet odour, under a dome of sapphire.

Another institution to go over is the great Government tobacco-factory, close by the Cathedral, where no less than five thousand women are employed. The sight is the workwomen. The process of cigar-making is as uninteresting as that of diamond-polishing, and yet one goes to witness both with far more anxious anticipation than to inspect what is far more remarkable—the making of a pin. The building in which the manufactory is carried on is a world in itself—an imposing oblong block, with a railed enclosure in front. Being Government property, it is guarded by soldiers, and the stranger is apt to take it, at first sight, for a gigantic barrack. The name of the king in whose reign it was erected (one of the Ferdinands) is still outside. The Republic has not ordered it to be erased, as a French Republic would have done before this. At Madrid I noticed the same delicacy, or forgetfulness, if you prefer it; the monogram and crown of Isabella were untouched on the lamp-posts in the most revolutionary quarters. The interior of the building consists of long whitewashed halls, divided into colonnades by rows of pillars, from which spring vaulted ceilings. The women are seated at low tables about two feet from the ground, in parties of half-dozens. They were there of every age, from the tawny hussy of sixteen to the fully developed matron with her infant tumbling in a cradle beside her, and the wrinkled hag with her iron-grey locks bound with a gay bandana. Poor, but merry and impudent withal, they were; and some of the sprightly hoydens, with sprays of lilac and rosebuds in their magnificent ebon hair, were a little too ready with a wink. There is a tradition that they smoke, not dainty cigarettes, but full-flavoured cigars; in any case, they are carefully searched before leaving to see that they do not smuggle out any trabucos for personal consumption or as gifts to their favoured swains. They were dressed invariably in lively cotton prints, with short shawls of red, or crimson, or saffron, or other hue outvying the tulip in garishness. To be shockingly frank, not one of them was conspicuously pretty; they had brilliant eyes and teeth, but all had an ill-fed, dried-up appearance, even those who were inclined to flesh. The Spanish woman, after a certain age, has a tendency to get fat without passing through the buxom stage; connoisseurs pretend that this is the combined effect of rancid oil and sweetstuff. But it is not gallant to dive into the secrets of female nature. Very assiduously these "lazy Andalusiennes" bent to their tasks, picked and sorted the leaves, rolled the cigars into shape, clipped them, gummed the ends, and packed them into bundles tied with smart ribands of silk; for they are paid by the piece, and the bull-fighting season is near, and they must save the price of a seat at the corrida on Easter Sunday, come what will. The cigars are assorted in boxes according to their shape and size, their brand and their strength, the latter being indicated by the words "claro," "claro colorado," "colorado" (which is the medium flavour), "colorado maduro" and "maduro" as they advance in five gradations from mild to strong. Leaving the cigar-hall, I was shown into the cigarette-hall, where a number of quieter girls, with shallow boxes of tobacco-dust almost as fine as snuff before them, were rolling the paper cylinders exactly as it is done by smokers, but with fingers surer and nimbler. In another hall the cartuchos, or packages to hold cigarettes and tobacco, were made. They were ready printed and cut, waiting to be put on a wooden frame, turned over, and pasted. One child of ten was pointed out to me as the quickest in the lot. Her small hands flew over her work with a rapidity that dazzled. She had need to be expeditious, poor wean, for she received just one farthing for every hundred packages she made!

There are others besides the tantalizing tile-makers and the saucy cigarreras who are rebellious to the drowsy influences of clime, and profanely work—the gipsies and the beggars. There are some of the former here, though not so many as in the pages of Murray. The excessively dirty and extremely picturesque race, with parchment skins and high cheek-bones, is dying out. A few stray members of the tribe remain in the remotest and raggedest part of the transpontine suburb, and shear mules, cope horses, and do tinkering jobs generally, filling in their spare time with petty larceny. Their women shuffle cards and tell fortunes. A splendid people they are, those gipsies—in Borrow's book and on canvas. In private life their society is not to be courted. If you do not want to see them, they are sure to turn up; if you do, as I did, you must look for them, and not always with success. I came across but one during my stay in Spain—a yellow girl who was eager to exhibit her palmistry at my expense in the immense coffee-house under the Fonda de Paris at Madrid—and she left a strong impression on my mind of having been own sister to a persuasive prophetess who once cozened me of half-a-crown on the towing-path at Putney at the 'Varsity boat-race on the Thames. Your hopes of assisting at a gipsy dance at Seville will be disappointed. If you give a courier two pounds sterling, he may be able to improvise you one; a pack of filthy, bony men and women will execute epileptic saltatory movements before you—not the Esmeralda dance, but lewd swaying of the body from the hips, and vehement contortions; and finally one creature will throw her handkerchief at your feet. A well-bred caballero will fill the handkerchief with shining dollars, and hand it back to her with a bow. This dance is work, downright hard work; but it is a dance for money. Mammon, not Terpsichore, is the genius to whom worship is paid. The mendicants toil as hard at their trade as those dancing gipsies. I counted fifty-seven in a short morning walk—some robust and some well-dressed, with the well-acted meekness of genteel poverty. The cripples, the deformed, the adults with baby arms and the jumping Billy-the-Bowls could not be paralleled out of South Italy. From the assortment could be furnished Burns's "Holy Fair" and the Pattern in "Peep o' Day" twice over, with something to leave. They are all past-masters and mistresses in the art of petitioning; they are professors of physiognomy like Lavater, and can tell at a glance a face which ought to belong to a charitable mortal; and then, what a command they have of the gamut of lungs, from the whine, the wheedle, and the snuffle, to the unctuous, droning prayer or the fierce malediction!

Still—beggars, gipsies, heat, and laziness to the contrary notwithstanding—Seville is delectable, and a marvel in its gardens and groves, its flowers and fruit, its fountains and fish-pools, its soft climate and soft people, its languorous repose and silvery tinkles to prayer. Seville is romance. Shall it ever be mine again to lie beneath the shade of its secular orange-trees, and blink at clustering shafts of marble tipped with silver sun-rays, and dream dreams? As I write, methinks to my ear rises the cry of the guardian of the night, the last I heard as I left, half warning, half supplication: "Ave Maria Purissima, las diez han dado."

END OF VOL. 1.

FOOTNOTES:

[A] In fair play to Santa Cruz, it is right to state that he believed this female to be a spy, who, under the pretence of Carlism, was willing to "betray the volunteers of God and the King, and carried despatches to the enemy sewn up in her dress." Still, the idea of a minister of religion ordering a woman to be shot does not recommend itself, although the woman may have justly deserved her fate.

[B] The Duke de Sanlucar is an O'Shea. I hope he is a relative of mine; for kinship with a grandee, however distant, is something to brag about. We always speak of our exalted connections. One never hears me dropping a syllable of a cousin of mine who was a bounty-jumper in the United States, agent-in-advance to a nigger-minstrel troop, and subsequently drove a butcher's cart in Brooklyn. He was a fearful, but most fascinating ruffian.

Booksophile
Your Local Online Bookstore

Buy Books Online from
www.Booksophile.com

Explore our collection of books written in various languages and uncommon topics from different parts of the world, including history, art and culture, poems, autobiography and bibliographies, cooking, action & adventure, world war, fiction, science, and law.

Add to your bookshelf or gift to another lover of books - first editions of some of the most celebrated books ever published. From classic literature to bestsellers, you will find many first editions that were presumed to be out-of-print.

Free shipping globally for orders worth US$ 100.00.

Use code "Shop_10" to avail additional 10% on first order.

Visit today
www.booksophile.com

www.ingramcontent.com/pod-product-compliance
Lightning Source LLC
Chambersburg PA
CBHW020206090426
42734CB00008B/957